*To my dear friends Paul and Eddie,*

*Hope this book touches your heart,*

*Love,*

*Janis*

# HOW TO BE
## HEALTHY WEALTHY HAPPY

*Other Books by Raymond Charles Barker*

MONEY IS GOD IN ACTION

THE POWER OF DECISION

THE SCIENCE OF SUCCESSFUL LIVING

SPIRITUAL HEALING FOR TODAY

TREAT YOURSELF TO LIFE

TREATMENT: WHAT IT IS AND HOW TO DO IT

YOU ARE INVISIBLE

COLLECTED WISDOM OF
RAYMOND CHARLES BARKER

# How to Be
# HEALTHY
# WEALTHY
# HAPPY

RAYMOND CHARLES BARKER

**DeVorss Publications**
*Camarillo, California*

**How to Be Healthy Wealthy Happy**
Copyright © 1986 by First Church of Religious Science, New York
Previously released as: Collected Essays of Raymond Charles Barker

ISBN-10:     0-87516-578-8
ISBN-13: 978-0-87516-578-3
Library of Congress Control Number: 86-71939


Fourth Printing, 2006

DeVorss & Company, Publisher
P.O. Box 1389
Camarillo CA 93011-1389
w w w . d e v o r s s . c o m

Printed in the United States of America

# Contents

These essays were originally
published as separate booklets.

# Spirit, Soul and Body

*Everything begins as an idea in Mind, moves through the process of consciousness, enters into a Law of action, and completes itself in a tangible form known as demonstration.*

## WHAT IS SPIRIT?

THE UNIVERSE IS evidence of God. The universe could not be self-created, any more than man is. You are in a God-Mind which is always greater than you are. It always knows more than you do.

A friend said to me the other day, "As I listen to you lecture I do not have a sense of the Presence of God, because you are

1

always telling us the mechanics of the Law of Mind.'' Perhaps by constantly telling people in practical language that metaphysics works, I forget the Thing which makes it work. You can be so interested in the carburetor of your car that you forget it is in an automobile. You think of it as merely a carburetor.

There is an impelling force for good. It is God. It is in all, through all and equally distributed in every person. Its main characteristics are intelligence and love. It is inspiration and warmth, but It is also mechanical Law. There is an overshadowing Presence which is always with you. It is the primary, loving, creative action of Life. You are always in It. It is always in you. It is always working for your good. It is always desiring the best for you. God wants you to be happy, healthy and to have love and self-expression.

Why do you believe this? You have need of these things. The very need of them indicates their naturalness to you. Anything natural to you is a part of Life, a part of God. You are in a Power which is always evolving you a bit higher. You are in a Mind whose essential nature of love and unity maintains you as a whole person. It is seeking to keep you from being hurt by the accidents of life. There is an overall Mind which acts around you and through you yet is always greater than you are. At the same time, God acts in you in a personal way. This is Spirit.

One of our great writers, Thomas Troward,* states that the difference between Spirit and matter is that Spirit has Intelligence as its key characteristic and matter has form as its key characteristic. All ideas are produced by a Thinker. The Thought which It thinks produces a Form in which the Thought becomes obvious. That is the trinity—a Divine Thinker, a Spiritual Thought and a Form in substance. Mind, idea and manifestation.

---

*See Chapter 1 of Troward's *The Edinburgh Lectures on Mental Science.*

You are in an eternal Process of thinking. What you think must by its own nature become a form. We used to say that thoughts are things. They are not. Thoughts are not things, they *cause* things. Things are not thought, things are the result of thought. Whether it is your television or your automobile, it is not a thought; it is a thing resulting from an idea.

But there could not be a thing if there had not been a thought. Things do not create themselves. Back of every "thing" is an idea. Behind the Cosmic order in which you live is an Infinite Thinker. The Thought which It thinks is a good Thought, a creative Thought and a loving Thought.

Spirit denotes a universal Presence, in which you are forever immersed. It is a Presence of Intelligence and an action of Love. It knows what to do and It wants to do it. When you love someone, you want to do something for him. The universe is the visibility of a knowing Mind, an impersonal yet compassionate Love, an endless Goodness and an eternal Possibility. That is Spirit.

These are also qualities of yourself. You are right in assuming that you are Spirit. You have a definite presence, a definite mind. You love to create. You see results take form in your life. The Universal Spirit is always in man, and man is always Spirit in his individual use of life.

Spirit indicates a free-flowing, creative, non-repetitive Action in the universe and in man. Therefore, in you there is an eternal uniqueness. In you is a quality which is not in any other living soul. It never has been and never will be. There is something about you that is peculiar to you. This something has the power to maintain you as an original, unique person. No matter what may be done to make people look alike, act alike or think alike, it never succeeds. Uniformity is an utter impossibility. There is a quality in the individual which you can never regiment.

Something created you. If it was not a Man-God, then what was It? Was it merely evolution? No. Evolution can never be completely explained until you know why life evolves. Evolution is a process of continual refinement. What causes this refining? A mechanical law? No, because the process is too intelligent. It knew enough to take floating protoplasm in the swamp and develop it into a fish, the fish into the animal, and the animal into the man. A mechanical law would not know how to do that.

An automobile operates as mechanical law. The automobile does not know how to go from your home to your office. It has to have a conscious intelligence operating it. A mechanical law cannot operate without Intelligence directing it. Man could not have evolved out of nothing.

The Mind which evolved him knew what It was doing before It started to do it. You have evolved out of God. Evolution can be explained by science, but why evolution is, science cannot explain. Science can tell you why it works, but it cannot tell you what it is. Psychology has never yet discovered why you think and feel. It only knows the problems which arise from your thinking and feeling.

Science explains the automatic side of life, but it does not explain the spontaneous side of life. Medicine may determine your degree of health, but it cannot explain why you are healthy. One person interviewed at ninety-eight years of age declares that he is healthy because he never smoked or drank alcohol and ate a modest amount of food, attributing his longevity to this regime. Another elderly man reports that he drank a pint of whiskey a day, smoked ten cigars a day, ate what he pleased and has lived to be 102.

The outer will never explain the inner. Any definition of you as body, as what you do, where you go, people you know, or your bank account doesn't define you. It defines what you do with your life but not what you are.

You are always the living Spirit Almighty. Man is always greater than what he appears to be, because a Divine Idea projects every person.

In Jesus' time, the land now called Israel was divided into three sections, like three counties. Looking at a map you would note that the top section was Galilee, the center section Samaria and the bottom section Judea. Jesus did most of his teaching in Galilee. Three times each year he went to Jerusalem for the annual festivals of the Jews, and Jerusalem was in Judea. Like all orthodox Jews of his day, he never went through Samaria, because no Jew went through Samaria. The religious differences and mixed marriages of the Samaritans made them outcasts and their country hated.

In the 4th chapter of John it says, "And he must needs go through Samaria," meaning he couldn't help himself, for he was in a hurry. Every Jew traveling from Galilee to Jerusalem went forty miles out of his way to go around Samaria. When you walk forty miles it is quite a distance, yet thousands of pilgrims from Galilee would go around Samaria to avoid being contaminated by the Samaritans.

It must have been an event for Jesus to pass through this section, because the Bible says, "And he must needs go through Samaria" (John 4:4). Taking the shorter route, he came to a village which was the last remnant of what had once been the great ancient city of Samaria. He came to it tired and worn and stopped at the village well.

Here took place the famous story of the woman at the well. Sitting by the side of the well talking to her, he looked into the distance and beheld a famous mountain, the second most famous mountain in all of Palestine—Mt. Gerizim. They built a huge gold-plated, gem-studded temple, trying to outdo the great temple to the south of them. In the passing years their own temple had fallen into decay as their country had not prospered, yet thousands of Samaritans in Jesus' day still visited it for the annual feasts.

As he was talking with the woman at the well, she said, "Our fathers worshipped in this mountain, and ye say that in Jerusalem is the place where men ought to worship." Jesus replied, "Woman, believe me, the hour cometh when ye shall neither in this mountain nor yet in Jerusalem worship the Father. . . . But the hour cometh, and now is, when the true worshippers shall worship the Father in spirit and in truth, for the Father seeketh such to worship him. God is Spirit; and they that worship him must worship him in Spirit and in Truth."

As you grow mentally and spiritually, you evolve out of the necessity of things, into the need for great ideas. You develop a consciousness where you see that form, while necessary, is merely the product of an idea and that the Mind which creates is always greater than the form It creates.

We work in Spirit and in Truth, so there is not loyalty to a building, nor to person, nor to a creed. Our faith is in a Universal Mind, Presence, Power and Creative Urge—in us, around us, always greater than we are. It impels us toward greatness. It says, "Use me, know me." It says, "You are greater than you think." It says, "Come up higher."

Spirit in you is God individualizing Himself as you. It is your conscious mind knowing God aright.

## WHAT IS SOUL?

I LIKE TO ASK embarrassing questions. I often ask people who know nothing of Truth, "What is your soul?" I have never yet had a clear answer. They usually reply that they must have one, but they aren't at all sure what it is or where it might be located in them. They think it goes with them after death—at least they hope so. We should be able to give a clear answer to this question, because the word "Soul" has a simple explanation.

God is Life, and there is a certain way life acts. God is Love, and there is a definite way love acts. God is Power, and there is a way power acts. There is one Mind and a way in which It creates. Soul is neither a location nor a thing in and of itself. It is a way mind acts.

The law of electricity is not electricity, nor is it the light which electricity gives. Yet electricity without a law wouldn't give light. The law of electricity is the way it works. You have a mind, and there is a way in which your mind works. Your soul is the way your mind works.

As you study the Mind of God and Its operation, you discover a creative Law operating it. There is a Creative Power which acts as Mind, just as there is a Creative Power which acts as nature. This Power acts in you when you think. How do I know? Because what you think affects you. When you are happy you think one way and are glad. When you are unhappy you think another way and are depressed. Thought has within it a creative element which must act in the way you direct it.

All life is the interplay of thought and feeling resulting from the forces and influences of life—the home, business, recreation, friends, family. Life is the action of mind through emotion, producing form and resultant situations. Your soul is the way in which you function. You are a living soul, a living channel through which Mind thinks, a Law acts and a result is produced. Life is a thinking Mind, immersed in a feeling Law, producing tangible results.

There is an originating Center in the mind of each of us which is Spirit. It is one with the originating Power, which is everywhere evenly distributed and which we call God. Spirit is the action of a universal Mind, which is all knowledge, all wisdom and all intelligence, focalizing Itself in and through the individual in a unique and distinct way.

You will always be you, wherever you are. Anyone who ever was is still being himself somewhere. You are what you are because there is something in you which prevents you from ever being anything else. Spirit is the unique quality of the individual. It is individuality. That is why you are different from others. No matter with whom you live, associate or play, you will never be like them nor will they ever be like you. This explains why all methods of regimentation have failed. No decrees of group legislation succeed at the level of the individual. They cannot. Everyone must be free to be himself, as long as he works in the general structure of the culture and society in which he is functioning.

Religion, if it is effective, must be related directly to the individual, not to a group. You do not achieve heaven on the basis of the church you attend. You evolve on the basis of what you, as an individual, do with yourself. You are your own future. You are the only one who determines what the next twenty or more years are going to be for you. You are the only thinker in your world. No other person thinks as you do.

This spiritual uniqueness is your basis of freedom. You are born in the image and likeness of God. You are born in the image and likeness of a Mind which forever differentiates Itself yet never standardizes Itself. Whatever the Creative Power is, It is forever producing new and varied things. Yet It never repeats and has never produced two things alike. In a crowd we may all look alike, but as we observe each individual, we see something unique. Life will always be that way. When you try to be like anyone else, you forfeit your divine inheritance. If you try to please others by aping the patterns in which they function, you are doomed.

You must be yourself—that is Spirit. But what you do with what you are is Soul. The *way* you think, the *way* you react, the *way* you adjust is Soul. Soul is the subconscious area of mind. You think consciously, but you respond subconsciously. There is no such thing as a conscious physical action. Every action is actually a subconscious reaction. Your conscious mind decides what the action is to be, but it is your subconscious mind which executes it.

If someone says to you, "Meet me at Smith's Restaurant for dinner," you answer, "All right." Your conscious mind agrees. Your decision is made at the conscious level. Then all the intelligence, power, activity and coordination of the subconscious mind moves you to that restaurant. The subconscious does the actual work. You act with the conscious mind and react with the subconscious mind. You decide with the conscious, and the subconscious mind follows through.

That is the play of life upon itself. It is as old as consciousness. It is the way life is. A conscious idea accepted becomes a law to the subconscious mind to produce it.

Jesus emphasized the necessity of speaking and thinking constructively. He realized that when the conscious mind accepted an idea, the subconscious could only respond in like manner. He said to watch your words. What you talk about determines the tenor of your life, because your language always outpictures your mind.

Incidentally, your voice displays your consciousness. Your voice indicates to the world what you are really thinking. If you are too happy, it indicates hysteria. If you are depressed, it indicates melancholy. If you speak in a monotonous tone, it usually indicates inertia.

It is becoming increasingly difficult to be excited about a constructive idea. You get excited over a foreign country's actions. You get excited over income taxes. But it is difficult to get people excited about God or right thinking. It doesn't have a vital allure. Also, it doesn't have a threat. Many of the things which threaten you fascinate you. They make you think; they push you into action. When great ideas appear which do not threaten you, they do not find as deep a welcome within you. Try letting Divine Ideas come into consciousness and give them a hearty welcome and next give them embodiment. God's Ideas come to you without a threat.

The act of thinking causes something to happen. It directs a mental Law in you to cause something to happen. Unfortunately, today most people think of the subconscious mind as merely the repository of neuroses. Popular misinformation has made the subconscious mind a negative, destructive force. True, the causes of your troubles are the patterns in the subconscious; but that is only one phase of subconscious operation. It is only one of thousands of activities which are managed by the subconscious. The subconscious digests your food, directs your circulatory system and, in a word, operates you.

Every therapeutic technique has utilized a subconscious (soul) method. Man improves in direct ratio to the amount of positive, creative, forward-moving ideas functioning in him. He retrogresses in exactly the same ratio when his attention is diverted to the unpleasant, the difficult, the hard, the crude and the unlovely. That is why every great positive philosopher has talked about God, why religions have developed.

Is there a positive, creative way of living? Yes. How do you know this? Because every Bible has said so? Because every prophet, Messiah and Spiritual Teacher has announced it? These are proof to many. Mainly, you know it is so because you are doing it. You are in the midst of creative living. You are making a serious attempt to be optimistic when the average person is pessimistic. You realize that the subconscious mind is not merely a repository of troubles. It is a great creative mechanism designed by an Intelligence which knows far more than you do.

Anyone reading today's psychology should be impelled to think of a Divine Mind. The more you study the way the human mind works, the more you realize that it, as a human mind, could not create itself. Unlimited potentials are resident in even the most warped subconscious. A psychotherapist not merely straightens out a neurotic pattern; he also releases a plus element which rises to the surface as a creative activity. The individual is healed not merely by the rearrangement of subconscious patterns, but by the creative element which acts once the rearranged patterns permit it freedom of movement.

Every field of modern scientific investigation leads to the necessity of a belief in an Infinite Mind, an Infinite, Creative Intelligence, an Infinite Life, which no matter what you do with It, still continues on Its way, in Its own perfect order. With It you may synchronize yourself, as, when and if you so desire. That is why every religion has said that no matter how depraved, how far on the negative side of life man is, he can always make a comeback.

Theologians have called the process salvation, redemption and regeneration. They are saying that a rearrangement of the basic drives, motives and patterns of life can take place at any time, and anyone can rise out of the mediocrity of his own past, into the creativity of his own present, and look forward to the further possibilities of his own future. You can do this; anyone can do this. That is the way life is. Otherwise, there would be no reason for any form of healing. If this weren't so, we should give up the medical, psychological and spiritual fields of healing. Medicine does not heal; it prepares the patient for healing. Psychology does not heal; it prepares the patient for healing. And metaphysics does not heal; it prepares the patient for healing.

Any system you use which enables you to be a creative person will work. They are all good. We have no arguments with medicine or with psychology. However, we particularly believe in spiritual mind healing through our methods. All healing methods are good, because they are doing exactly the same thing. They are using different soul techniques.

What is your soul? Your soul is that phase of the subconscious which takes your thought, creates an emotional pattern to back it up and produces it into a form. Spirit is what you are. Soul is the way you work. You are a thinker, and when you think, something happens to what you think. The thinking is Spirit, the happening is Soul. You exist as a thinking individual in a field of subjective soul response.

The Psalmist wrote, "Bless the Lord, O my soul, and all that is within me, bless his holy name. Forget not his benefits, who forgiveth all thine iniquities, healeth thy diseases and redeemeth thy life from destruction." He said in essence, "I acknowledge a creative Power in the universe and in myself, which is God. It is Spirit and It is Truth. My soul now acts in accordance with God. The negatives of my life fall away and the positives of my life are established."

He who is able to see his present mind as a spiritual process, a living spiritual organism, can deliberately use it for his good. You are the sum total of all that you have known yourself to be through the years: all your experiences, all your pressures, all your plans, all your aspirations, all the events which have come upon you. This aggregation is a part of your soul. Yet soul is more than that. It is more than memory, because it knows how to individualize what you know you are. The great have said, "I am the Spirit of God," and they became great because their souls (their subconscious) made them great. Other people have said, "I am a failure" and became failures because their souls took them at their own word. If a person says, when a loved one dies, "I'll never be happy again," the soul acts by maintaining that person in the desolation of sorrow. Always, the soul must do what the conscious mind directs it to do. When the conscious mind does not deal with creative ideas, then the subconscious mind has no creative urge in it; it has been given no creative thing to do.

"Many are called, but few are chosen." Millions have had an inner impulse to do something creative. Only a few thousand have followed through and accomplished it. The millions say, "But I can't"; the few say, "I will." You are either on one side of life or on the other. You can sit back and say, "I will endure to the end." Or you can say, "What can I do within myself that is creative, so that my soul can cause a creative event to happen in my life?"

## WHAT IS BODY?

A QUESTION PEOPLE OFTEN ask me is "What is the material world?" Theology has implied that the world is a dangerous place. The orthodox churches teach that the world is a place of hard work, that sin lurks at every corner and the devil will lead you astray. Do Religious Scientists believe this? No.

As you define the word "Body," you think of the physical body which you use every day. You also use "Body" in a larger sense. You speak of a body of people, or a body of nations, meaning an interrelated group with a common denominator. It is in that sense that I use the term, for I believe that all form is body. Anything which has outline is body. Anything with the quality of matter is body. There is little difference between the human body and any other form in the universe.

Spirit is conscious expression of life as mind and intelligence. In man it is volition or will. Soul is the way Spirit works. It works through the conscious and subconscious mind. It works through you as a thinking, feeling organism. Body is the result of Spirit working through Soul, producing form. It is that simple.

We are in an Infinite Presence, which is God. There is an eternal Mind which is always creating, always new, even when your present world seems stale. Often, things which are usually pleasant and cheery experiences, and which have been inspirational, are suddenly dulled. Life becomes stale. Yet Life in itself is never stale. God is an endless beginning. It is an endless freshness, an endless creativeness, which is pouring Itself out upon you, through you, around you, for God is the sum total of all creation. It is infinity and eternity. God is the inescapable, the inevitable.

There is a Divine Intelligence, a Divine Pattern, a Divine Plan, a Divine Immensity in which you are forever immersed, and which is forever in action in you and through you. This Divinity is so magnificent that It will never be completely defined or completely understood. Yet you are able to understand and define the action of God as It works through you.

You cannot know God in His immensity but you can know Him in your mind, heart, body and in the affairs of the day. Intelligence governs, Law creates, a Process takes place. Creation is always happening. God in the Infinite you can only surmise. You are your own philosopher. But God where you are, you can know. You are alive; you think; you are.

This Divine Immensity is forever giving of Itself. Spirit is forever saturating you with the inspiration of Its own being. It acts through you at the level of your own mind, your own thoughts, your own feelings. As you experience It, and as you direct It (consciously or not), It produces form. What it produces can be defined as body.

Body is constantly being made new. It is an ever-renewing process. Thousands of cells are born each day, and thousands die each day. That is the process. In a church, the pulpit, the platform, the flowers, the chairs are a part of body. Mind is always creating ideas, producing ideas, and new forms are always appearing. Body change is necessary as is change at any other level.

God is never the same. One of the negative characteristics of the human mind is to want things to remain the same. The Infinite is forever in process of change. Looking at a sunset or at any other form of Nature, you see constant change. Body as Nature is always in change. Yet people want their bodies to stay youthful all the time. They would like always to look twenty-five. They would like things around them to remain at a permanent point.

Mind will always change, and form will always change. You might as well adjust to it. Live in a changing world of form and realize that it is natural, normal and necessary. Ideas appear; the Soul, the Law, creates them into form; and forms appear in order to disappear. Spirit, in the form of ideas, acts in the Infinite Mind to produce ideas in order to dissolve ideas. The Soul, which is the Law, the Process, formulates the idea in order to dismiss the idea. Body, the manifest form of the idea, endures long enough to reveal itself and then disintegrates.

At every Sunday morning service our church has fresh flowers. They appear as Body, fulfill their function and disintegrate. Ideas appear, are formulated and disappear. That is why, metaphysically speaking, any claim on the past is not spiritual. Ideas arise in the Spirit. The Soul, your subconscious, produces them. They take form, endure for a time, and go on their way.

Very few people live flexibly. Everything appears in your world in order to disappear from your world, because something greater will appear in order to disappear. You may say negatively, "Then every good thing which comes to me will leave me." Yes, it will. But "Angels go out of my world to let archangels come in." Every good appears, passes its time and moves out to let a greater good come in, pass its time and go out. If you linger in the halls of false memory and labor with the past, you have shut the door for a greater good to enter. The good of this moment is here; rejoice in it. It will move on its way. You cannot hold it. You cannot force it to remain. It will go to reveal a greater good. You may mourn, but your mourning delays the incoming of your next good.

People who mourn a loss of money do not make more money. Others lose money and casually say, "I'll make more money." And they do. Many are still mourning the money they lost in 1929. Others have made fortunes since 1929. One group stayed on the mourners' bench, the other group gave birth to new ideas.

Spirit, Soul and Body; the Infinite Presence offering Itself as Its own creation. Man, the means by which It gives itself into form through the Soul, is a living idea. The world around man is of his own creation, for he has fashioned it with ideas. Where did he get these ideas? They came from Spirit. You are in a building which originated as an idea in the mind of someone. It was then transmitted to the minds of a group. Construction appeared. It happened. This building is the result of an idea processed through the people.

Everything works this way. It always has, it always will. The Pyramids, the leaning Tower of Pisa, the Eiffel Tower, the Statue of Liberty, and the Empire State Building were built that way. In your world you may not have built buildings but you have built other forms. You have built a family, a home, an atmosphere into an apartment. Always, you are building the environment in which you are functioning, because you are Spirit, acting as Soul, producing Body. These three are an eternal changing, evolving, moving, flowing process. All Life is motion, action, movement from idea to form. You are the projector of your world of form. Ideas come to you every instant. You think them, you feel them, you produce them. Whether it be three meals a day or work in an office, you are projecting body. You are consciousness projecting form. Your business is a form of body. Your apartment is a form of body. Your personal associations are a form of body, because Body is that idea in Mind which gives outline to substance. You are forever doing this, and you can do it more wisely if you know the Law which does it.

This Science doesn't tell you anything that you are not already doing. It only informs you how you are doing it, so you can produce what you want. This teaching does not make you spiritual. There isn't a church in the world which can make you spiritual. If you can be made spiritual, then you aren't spiritual now. If you aren't now, you never will be. You are God's image now. Every person in the universe today is the complete operation of God. Every person is a thinking, creative inlet and outlet of the action of Infinite Mind, Infinite Spirit and Infinite Love. Knowing this, you live accurately with precision, discernment and specific results. You can say to one idea "No" and to another "Yes." You select what you would like to have happen and reject what you do not want.

Spirit, a Divine Thinker in the center of you. Soul, an orderly action which produces your thinking. Body, a result around you in form as obvious creation.

Everything in your world has become form because you, or

someone, thought it into form. When you go into your kitchen, every object is a result of an idea which someone somewhere thought into form. You use a knife, fork and spoon. You use stove, sink and refrigerator, yet there were thousands of years when there were no such conveniences. Someone had an idea. He thought upon the idea, he projected the idea.

Each is the inventor of the facts of his own experience. You are constantly receiving ideas, thinking ideas and producing ideas. You are the genius of your own world. You are God acting in the midst of flexible substance, projecting into your experience the ideas of your own mind. Do not worry when forms go out of your world. You can produce more. Worry only when your thinking processes are confused.

Do not fear the person who can take form from you. Rather, worry about the ideas which confuse your mind and your emotions. ''Fear not them that kill the body, but fear them that kill both body and soul.'' Worry not about your material world; concentrate on your mind. Spirit, the thinker; Soul, the actor; Body, the result. You are all three.

# God, Mind
# and Man

*Whatever you define God to be
is your definition of yourself.*

THESE ARE THREE key words in the study of practical
metaphysics. When you first heard of the Science of Mind, you
were either attracted or repelled by the fact that its followers
talked casually about God. You couldn't quite understand people who discussed God easily. You had been trained to think
of the Deity with great respect and awe. Then you heard a metaphysical speaker, or someone gave you a metaphysical book, and
you began to question your spiritual formality.

It dawned upon you that you were in a Presence, which is
one of intelligence and of life. You were in a Creative Process
which knew exactly what to do. Your new logical explanation

of life gave you a new God. Suddenly you had a larger viewpoint and a sense of spiritual ease which you did not have before.

Students of this teaching think of God as naturally as they think of anything else. It is natural to discuss God, to read about God, to think about God, to feel the presence of God. What would be unnatural to other people is to us completely natural.

Perhaps we have recaptured the naturalness which Jesus had in talking about God. He discussed It with ease and seemed to be completely at home with spiritual terminology. Yet they were terms quite different than others had used before him. He talked about the Father, the Spirit of Truth, and the Presence within him. Probably, the majority of his hearers thought he did not make much sense. To Jesus, though, all this made great sense, and those who followed him gradually found that the new words were better. They found that they not only made sense, they produced results. The more casual you are regarding the Presence, the Creative Process and the Mind of God, the more easily you make your spiritual demonstrations. It becomes second nature to you to respond to life in God's terms.

Any basic pattern introduced into the subconscious mind gradually produces an automatic reaction. Repeat an idea, study an idea, investigate an idea, and as you are indoctrinated by that idea, you automatically respond to it. It no longer requires a conscious response. It no longer requires you to think twice about it.

Here is an illustration: people in this country have been taught from childhood to rise when the "Star Spangled Banner" is played. We were taught this by our parents. As this music was played we stood quietly, put our shoulders back more than usual, and were respectful. Even in church, if the organist played the first two bars of the "Star Spangled Banner," we would stand up whether anyone asked us to rise or not, because that is our spontaneous reaction to the national anthem. We would not have to think about it, we would automatically rise, because it has become a subjective response in our mind.

It is equally possible to train yourself so that you have an automatic reaction to ideas of God when you need help. God is always where you are, and as you automatically react to It, It acts for you, by acting through you. They called Spinoza a God-intoxicated man, because he talked about God, wrote about God and thought about God all the time. They called him "the God-intoxicated man of Amsterdam." It had become his unconscious pattern to respond to every situation in terms of God.

What is this God whose pattern we deliberately implant in our subconscious? It is a God of intelligence, a God which is never static, a God of process, a God of movement, a God of flow, because the entire universe is movement. There is not a dead molecule, nor a static atom. There is not a cell in your body which is without rhythm, motion and intelligence. The Creator can be measured by His creation, just as you can measure creation in terms of the Creator. That which produces a universe must be Action. All that the physicists have discovered is further proof that the Creative Power is one of process, one of action. It knows what to do, is always doing it, and cannot be stopped in Its course. It cannot even be delayed. The only thing which is ever fooled by this is the human mind. I can say, "I do not like this chair, and I will destroy it." I may throw it in a furnace and burn it, but I haven't destroyed anything except my concept. Every particle of the chair has merely translated its fundamental intelligence, energy and form into another area called heat, light, smoke and ashes. I have fooled myself in my attempt to destroy Intelligence. You cannot destroy It, because Intelligence is Mind, the Spirit of God in action.

The word "Spirit" denotes action. It denotes Intelligence moving into form. It defines something being created, produced and formulated. Our God is a God of perfect intelligent action. God as Presence acts as Mind. All life is the movement of Mind and ideas. In this Science you become increasingly aware of the power of thought and feeling. Ideas and moods dominate you for hours, days, weeks or seconds. Ideas and feeling are cause, and realizing they are cause, you handle them at the mental level of causation.

As you become interested in consciousness (in thought and feeling), you begin to judge people more on the premise of what they think and feel than by what they have and what they seem to be. You also judge yourself on that same basis. What are you thinking? What is this feeling that you have? Is it good? If it is, you will maintain it; if it isn't, then you will discard it. As you become Mind-conscious, you become mood-conscious.

The most overrated thing in your world is your opinion of yourself. The human ego decreases with the perception that you are God's Idea appearing in a mind-process with a purpose governed by intelligence. The more you think of yourself as spiritual man, the more the human ego deflates itself. You perceive that you as a person are not very important, but that you as an individual are the appearance of a Divine generic idea, a universal idea. You behold yourself as an individual in a universal Presence, always individualizing that Presence, always personalizing that Presence with a purpose born of the ages.

Think of yourself as spiritual man, and cease thinking of yourself in terms of name, age, bank account and social position. Think of yourself in terms which are creative. Realize that you are the creation of an Infinite Spirit, a Divine Mind, and a Holy Law. Know that within you is Something capable of being greater than you are at this moment. Begin to think of yourself in larger terms.

A larger concept of God gives you a larger concept of Mind, which in turn gives you a larger concept of yourself. The absolute metaphysician knows that nothing in this universe needs to be changed except as a concept. There is nothing wrong with any person with whom you associate that a change of concept or consciousness will not cure.

We are immersed in an Infinite Mind, which is God. We are in It, and It is in us. We are in It with a purpose, a plan and a possibility. We are in God with a Divine Design and a Divine Pattern. Those who let Truth operate this pattern in them are the people who improve the world. Great people allow themselves to become the vehicles of an idea. Jesus' greatness lay in his ability to let an Idea act through him. He gave God freedom of action. "The Father that dwelleth in me, he doeth the works" (John 14:10). Jesus knew that he was motivated by a Divine purpose, was immersed in a perfect Presence, and was governed by God's Intelligence. He let God in the midst of him flow out from him and operate around him. Those who accepted his ideas were healed. The others scoffed and continued to make more money, to build more houses, to dust more funiture and to have more mortgages.

Average people are so accustomed to this three-dimensional world of form and shape that it is beyond their ability to conceive of something greater than the physical and tangible. They are incapable of believing in a prosperity not measured in terms of money. They are incapable of believing in a health not measured in terms of how long they can work before getting tired, how late they can stay up at night and not be weary the next morning. If they are sick, there is a good doctor nearby, so why do they need God?

God, Mind and Man. A universal creative Presence. A Mind

which is the way It acts, and Man who is the means by which It individualizes Itself into form on this plane.

> *That the righteousness of the law*
> *might be fulfilled in us, who walk not*
> *after the flesh, but after the Spirit.*
>
> *For they that are after the flesh do mind*
> *the things of the flesh; but they that are*
> *after the Spirit the things of the Spirit.*
>
> *For to be carnally minded is death; but*
> *to be spiritually minded is life and*
> *peace.*
>
> *Because the carnal mind is enmity*
> *against God: for it is not subject to the*
> *Law of God, neither indeed can be.*
>
> *So then they that are in the flesh cannot*
> *please God.*
>
> *But ye are not in the flesh, but in the*
> *Spirit, if so be that the Spirit of God*
> *dwell in you.*
>
> *For as many as are led by the Spirit of*
> *God, they are the sons of God.*
>
> —Romans 8:4–9, 14

Paul implies that you have two ways of looking at life. You view it either as a spiritual action or as a material action. If you view it as a material action, you may make more money, be more successful and influence more people, but you will probably have ulcers, later in life a touch of arthritis, and finally something which will carry you off this plane.

We believe in the Spirit of God in man. We believe that it is logical to live with wisdom, to know life as God's action, to feel love as an Infinite eternal togetherness, to be in the flesh but to use it as a vehicle and not as an end. We are not carnally minded, we are spiritually minded. We are interested in living God's Life now. There is only one Infinite Presence, God, acting as one Infinite Mind; God, forever individualizing Itself as perfect Man, the Son of God. Those who have eyes to see this live as spiritually minded people in a flexible universe, in health, in peace of mind and in a sense of security. Those who do not have eyes to see this live the other way. I trust that in the weeks to come you will live in a flexible universe made of Spirit, seeing all things as good, living with Intelligence, producing good works and loving one another.

# Treatment

*Correct mental work is scientific prayer. It is man's spiritual life insurance.*

## INTRODUCTION

My SEVERAL DECADES of ministry in the metaphysical field have convinced me that the greatest gift which we have to offer the world is the science of correct mental work, which we call *treatment* or *scientific prayer*. It is our only means of changing consciousness spiritually, and only the students who know how to give themselves treatments will prove our teachings. The others will listen, read and remain at the same level of thought as they were when they first came to our doors. Our Movement has been greatly hampered by sincere people who believed in Truth but who failed to learn how to treat and therefore failed to make demonstrations.

This booklet contains the essence of a series of Class Lessons which I have given in New York City in the past few years, and which I shall continue to give as long as I am an active worker in Truth. They are simple, easy to understand and give definite suggestions on methods of treatment. Anyone willing to experiment with the material outlined herein and willing to devote fifteen minutes a day to its practice will change himself for the better. There is no question in my mind regarding this, for I have seen people transform their lives by using these techniques.

Much of the material in this book is not mine. It is rather a compilation of the best I have read, studied, practiced and taught for many years. I am especially indebted to the following teachers who have meant much to me along the way and from whose teachings and writings I have taken material to formulate this concise booklet: Ernest Holmes, Thomas Troward, F. L. Rawson, Charles Fillmore and Elizabeth Carrick-Cook. They have helped to make abstract Truth practical.

I am knowing that all readers will find the Truth of themselves as they work with the ideas in this booklet. The Infinite Mind within will reveal to them the joy of correct mental work based upon principles which never fail, for they are not of men— they are of God by means of men.

# LESSON NO. 1

## Definitions

*Treatment is definite spiritual thinking within ourselves, upon ourselves, about ourselves, to change ourselves.* (RCB)

*A treatment is a conscious movement of thought, and the work begins and ends in the thought of the one giving the treatment.* (Holmes, *The Science of Mind*, p. 171)

*Treatment is the science of inducing, within Mind, concepts, acceptances and realizations . . . of whatever the particular need may be.* (Holmes, *The Science of Mind*, p. 164)

FIRST STEP IN TREATMENT:

### Define the Nature of God

Make statements about God. Declare what you believe God to be in your own terms. Write out a list of synonyms for God. Speak these definitions aloud and rapidly as often as you can. Remember that you already have a vocabulary and an ability to describe evil in every possible way. By defining God and lengthening your list daily, you are soon able to build a vocabulary to describe God, the Good, Omnipotent. Words are important. Get a flow and an ease in making audible statements of Truth.

### Example of Treatment

There is only one Mind, God, Infinite Good, Infinite Love, Infinite Truth. This Mind rules and governs all. This Mind is my mind now. The Life, Love and Mind of God are in action in me at this instant. I am filled completely with the Light and Spirit of Truth.

Through my mind God thinks. Through my heart God expresses Divine Love. Through my body God expresses His perfect life, health and vitality. There is no life, truth, substance or intelligence in evil; God, the Good, is all there really is, and I am surrounded and filled with It. In my life God is the only activity now taking place.

I have spiritual wisdom, spiritual perception and spiritual discernment. I love Truth, speak Truth, rejoice in Truth, for God is Truth. Amen.    (R.C.B.)

### Treatment for Divine Guidance

God is Mind, and this perfect Intelligence is now acting in me, through me, and for me. This perfect God-Mind created me and is the thinking capacity within me. I know that in Divine Mind is the answer to every question and the fulfillment of every need. I am now definitely inspired to right action in my life by the Ideas of the Spirit which are acting in my consciousness. I know what to do, when to do it and how to do it. I am open and receptive to God's guidance, God's wisdom and God's Love. I rejoice in my sure faith in this inner wisdom, and I am successful in all my ways.    (R.C.B.)

# LESSON NO. 2

## Definitions

*There isn't God and man, there is only God as man, and I am that now.*   (R.C.B.)

*The foundation for correct mental treatment is perfect God, perfect man, and perfect being. Thought must be organized to fit this premise, and conclusions must be built on this premise.* (Holmes, *The Science of Mind*, p. 159)

SECOND STEP IN TREATMENT:

### Define Yourself As a Spiritual Being

After taking the first step (defining the nature of God), we now begin to affirm the spiritual reality of man. Just as you have made a series of statements about the Divine Mind, now make a series of statements about yourself as a Son of God, a spiritual being. This series of statements should be as many as those dealing with God. Think of all that you know about the spiritual possibilities of man. All the attributes you have given God can now be given to yourself. All that is true of God is true of man. Do this daily until you are free and easy in the doing of it. You are injecting great and new ideas into your area of consciousness, and this is effective treatment. You are only cleaning up your own ideas about yourself.

### Example of Treatment

There is only one Mind, God, Infinite Good, and man is made in the image and likeness of God. I am a perfect being in a perfect world, governed by a perfect God. I express divine wis-

dom, intelligence and knowledge. When I speak, God speaks;
God speaks by means of me, for I am God's consciousness. I
am forever individualizing infinite power, the infinite power of
infinite love. I am spiritual and perfect now, for there is nothing but God and His infinite manifestation.

I am Spirit, I am Love, I am Life. All that God is, I am. The
full Mind, Life and Love of God are now in action in me and
through me. I am a perfect Idea in the Mind of God, and all
power is given unto me. There is no evil in my world, for
through me Good alone rules and governs my life. I am Divine,
and I speak Truth, live Truth, radiate Truth, for this is all there
really is. Amen.    (R.C.B.)

## Treatment for Health

God is the health of His people. I believe that I am made
in the image and likeness of God. Therefore, this must include
perfect health, vitality, strength and normal activity. There is
nothing to fear, for God is the only power and the only presence
in my life. There is no fatigue, for the Life of God is my life,
and it cannot be depleted. It is an ever-renewing, ever-revitaliz-
ing action of spirit. There is no disease, no sickness, there is
only the perfect action of God in me as health. I know this, believe this and give thanks for this. It is true at this instant.
Amen.    (R.C.B.)

# LESSON NO. 3

## Definitions

*This present universe is the Kingdom of Heaven, and all we do is to clear away our misconceptions of It until we see It as It really is.* (R.C.B.)

*The practitioner is not trying to send out a thought, hold a thought, or suggest a thought. The practitioner is trying to realize the state of perfection of the patient.* (Holmes, *The Science of Mind*, p. 199)

*Every time you pray, your mind is permanently improved. By prayer alone can you alter the human mind, so if you pray without ceasing, it means constantly living in the presence of good instead of evil.* (Rawson, *Scientific Prayer*, p. 39)

THIRD STEP IN TREATMENT:

### Define This World As the Kingdom of Heaven

First, define God. Second, define spiritual man. Then make statements of Truth to convince yourself that this present world is the presence of God, the operation of Mind, and is alive with perfect Love. Erase all thinking of past and future and live in the present instant, the NOW. In this present split second God is all there is and there are no demonstrations to be made. It is the finished Kingdom. We don't go to It, for we are already in it. Time and space are nothing, and the perfect world of Reality is the Truth of this moment.

### Example of Treatment

There is nothing but God and His manifestation, and man is the full and complete expression of Mind. I am the consciousness of God, and through me all the Divine Ideas reveal themselves in my world. Wherever God is, there heaven is, and so I am in heaven at every instant, for I am always in the Divine Presence and conscious of the Infinite Mind. My present world is heaven, it is good, it is alive with Truth, Love and Perfection. There is no evil in my present experience, for God is where I am and is what I am. My heavenly world is filled with spiritual beings forever blessing and benefiting me. No man can hurt me, for Divine Love fills all the people in my world. Nothing can confuse me, for God is order, harmony and right action at every instant and in all places.

There is no past, nor future. Today is the day of the Lord. Today is the day of Completion. Today is the day of Demonstration. This moment is the only time there is, and this moment is saturated with God. It surrounds me, fills me and upholds me now and forevermore. I live, move and have my being in God's universe of Good.    (R.C.B.)

## Treatment For Prosperity

God is my unfailing, permanent and perfect supply. I do not work for a living, I work for the glory of God and the good of my fellowman. There is no lack, no limitation. God's Mind and Its perfect Ideas sustain me in all ways. I live in abundance, I rejoice in plenty, and I am prosperous in all my ways. God's money is mine to use for good, and I use it now with pleasure and wisdom.    (R.C.B.)

# LESSON NO. 4

## Definitions

*Exaggerated fear is a serious emotional problem and should be treated as definitely and as specifically as a disease. It can be minimized by clear treatment work. Fear is an insidious thing, and wise students treat daily to keep it under control.* (R.C.B.)

*Fear is the antithesis of Faith. It is the negation of confidence. Like Faith, fear may be conscious or subjective, and if it is to be eliminated, it must be removed both consciously and subjectively.* (Holmes, *The Science of Mind*, Glossary, p. 593)

FOURTH STEP IN TREATMENT:

### Deny Fear and Affirm Faith

This is one of the most vital parts in treatment and should be worked on daily. Every treatment you give yourself or another should include a denial of fear and an affirmation of faith. Make a strong denial of fear and follow this with a lengthy affirmation of faith. Be sure to follow all denials with several affirmations. This part of your treatment need not be lengthy, but it should be definite. In a case where the problem is one of exaggerated fear (neurosis), you would work against fear at great length, denying the particular form which the fear takes in the patient.

### Example of Treatment

I believe in God, the Good, omnipotent. I believe that God is a perfect Mind, Love, Law, Truth and Activity. I believe that

I am the creation of God and that I am the expression of all that Mind is. My world is God's world, heaven, right here and now.

There is nothing to fear, for I have absolute trust in God, the One Mind, in action in me and through me at every instant. I have no fear, for God is with me, for me and around me. Nothing can hurt me, depress me, impoverish me, or make me ill—there is nothing but God and His manifestation in my life at all times. I have faith in Good. I have faith in Divine Love. I have faith in the Power of Truth that is now working for my eternal good. I trust in the great law of Mind and its perfect operation. I am calm, poised and confident, for God alone rules and governs my life and affairs. I am free, praise God, I am free. (R.C.B.)

## Treatment for Success

My mind is a center of Divine operation. The Divine operation is always for expansion and fuller expression, and this means the production of something beyond what has gone before, something entirely new, not included in past experience, though proceeding out of it by an orderly sequence of growth. Therefore, since the Divine cannot change its inherent nature, it must operate in the same manner in me; consequently in my own special world, of which I am the center, it moves forward now to produce new conditions, always in advance of any that have gone before.  (Troward, The Doré Lectures on Mental Science, pp. 26–27)

# LESSON NO. 5

## Definitions

*A good practitioner handles each problem separately. A general statement of Truth will only get a general result. Specific mental work should be done on every phase of the case.* (R.C.B.)

*Practice is a definite statement in mind, a positive affirmation. It is an active, conscious, agressive mental movement and in such degree as it embodies an idea—and there is no longer anything in our minds which denies the idea—it will take form.* (Holmes, *The Science of Mind*, p. 277)

FIFTH STEP IN TREATMENT:

### Handling Each Symptom

Deny each symptom of the case separately and affirm a specific truth for each symptom. Always close your treatment with a strong statement of Love and Truth.

After following the four steps outlined, you then treat the individual case or situation. Make a list of all the negatives and be sure it covers every angle. Then deny each one separately and affirm the Truth for each symptom, using several affirmations for each if possible. Never make general statements such as "God is my health." Always deny the symptoms and affirm the opposites. Use the mental equivalents for the parts of the body. Remember, you are only treating consciousness, you never treat body. The greater your coverage of details, the more effective the treatment.

## Example of Treatment
### (Case of Cancer of the Stomach)

God is all there is. There is nothing but His One Mind and Its perfect action, forever producing, maintaining and re-creating this universe, which is heaven, right here and right now. I am the image and the likeness of God, and nothing can take place in me except the action of God, the action of Life. There is nothing to fear, for I have absolute trust in the Life, Health and perfect Action of God within me.

There is no cancer, there is only God—and God in action. There is no malignant growth, for only God's Ideas can grow in my thought and love. There is no pain. God's Presence in me, as me, is always ease, comfort and delight. The stomach represents man's capacity to assimilate God's Ideas, and therefore my consciousness is now absorbing and assimilating all of God's Ideas perfectly. No damage to the stomach, for God's pure Substance cannot be hurt or destroyed. All is perfect substance, perfect action and perfect form. There is no hurt to the ego, for God is my Identity. I am THAT I am which God is eternally knowing Himself to be. I am Spirit and I am Truth. I am the incarnation of God's Idea of Himself, and this idea cannot be eaten away, nor destroyed by a false belief. There is no cancer, there is only God's Love and Truth growing in my consciousness now and forever more. I know this, believe this, and accept this. It is the Truth right now at this instant.    (R.C.B.)

# LESSON NO. 6

## Definitions

*A treatment is a specific Cause placed in Mind. Having given the treatment, the responsibility of the practitioner ceases. At that instant the Law takes over and does the work. There is nothing further to do except to expect results. (R.C.B.)*

*We are not depending upon chance but upon the Law. The responsibility of setting the Law in motion is ours, but the responsibility of making It work is inherent in Its own nature.* (Holmes, *The Science of Mind*, p. 305)

SIXTH STEP IN TREATMENT:

### Place Your Treatment in the Law

Close every treatment with the statement that God does the work. This means we place it in the Law of Mind. We give the treatment, but the Law produces the treatment. If you like to also give thanks, do so, but be sure to give thanks that it is already done.

Jesus said that the Father in him did the work. This means that when our conscious mind has given the treatment, the subconscious takes over and brings forth the demonstration. We call this *placing it in the Law*. The Law of Cause and Effect is eternal, accurate and true. We are constantly using it unconsciously. When we treat, we use it consciously. No individual heals anyone; it is the Law that does the healing. God works in man as Law, the subconscious mind. These two phases of the One Mind working together produce all creation.

Treatment is active causation. As you treat, you are establishing a positive and definite cause in Mind, which the Law then takes and makes an effect. All treatments should be spoken or thought with a "punch." It should be a dynamic, joyous experience and should bring peace and faith to the one treating. Watch your flow of words, and constantly increase your vocabulary of spiritual terms. Keep adding new words to describe God, spiritual man, heaven and good. Become as free in your talking with Infinite Mind as you are in talking with a member of your own family. Give thanks that the work is already done, the demonstration already accomplished.

> *In the Center of the Circle*
> *Of the will of God I stand;*
> *There can be no second causes,*
> *All must come from His dear hand;*
> *All is well, for 'tis my Father*
> *Who my life has planned.*
>                                    Anonymous

## Final Suggestions

Treatment can be done anywhere, at any time, under any circumstances. However, to ensure results and to guarantee growth in spiritual understanding, it is advisable to assign a definite period each day for specific mental work. It is wise to cover the following points in your daily outline—fear, age, disease, lack and inharmony. Then add to your treatment whatever needs to be cleared for that day, always remembering that we deny the specific evil and affirm its opposite, the eternal positive (affirmation). Between these periods of daily meditation watch your thought constantly, and whenever a negative appears, stop it at once with a strong denial followed by an affirmation. To all error say, "There is not a word of Truth in it, and it never happened." Be faithful unto God, and His Glory shall be in you and shall come forth through you, bringing into manifestation your heart's desire.

> *May I so live in the Divine Spirit that all who contact me shall be healed; that all who contact my thought shall be blessed; and that whosoever has an evil thought against me shall be cleansed and, in that cleansing, find his good.*

# IN CONCLUSION

QUESTIONS ARE OFTEN asked regarding the differences between audible and silent treatment and whether one is more effective than the other. For myself, I have always found that audible treatment is more productive. Make your statements aloud, and rapidly. You will find that as you do this, your full attention will be given to the treatment, and all distractions will be shut out of your consciousness.

Naturally, there are times and places where audible treatment is either impossible or embarrassing, and in that event silent treatment is necessary. All treatment given with definite sincerity either audible or silent, will produce results, but a spoken treatment usually absorbs the full attention of the one treating and thus impresses the subconscious more easily.

Finally, the greater your sense of God, the greater your life will be. Consistent repetition of a Spiritual Idea eventually produces a demonstration. God responds to man as man thinks in terms of God.

# You Can

*We are Life and we have no adversary. There is no power in the world to prevent our demonstration.*

I BELIEVE THAT creation, the universe, you and I must have an affirmative reason for existence. I cannot believe that my physical body was created to be sick. I cannot believe that my mind was created to be either stupid or neurotic. I cannot believe that the world around me with its great capacity to produce good could be anything but a good world. Yet many people are always negative. They are certain they are going to be sick. They are certain they are going to be unhappy. They are certain their job won't work out. They are certain they are going to have financial strain. They live consistently in a world of negatives.

We need to remind ourselves that the universe is a spiritual system designed and created by an Infinite Wisdom and that you and I are spiritual beings capable of health, capable of ease, capable of intelligence, capable of functioning wisely in this good world of ours. We need this reminder. Often people say they don't need to go to church. That may be so. I don't know. I need to, because it reminds me of ideas which, during the past week, I have forgotten. It reminds me that life is essentially creative and valuable, that it can be lived in a way that is fruitful, that I can accomplish, that I can achieve, and that I can become. Whether I read the Old Testament or the New, or the writings of other great teachers, they all assure me of the same thing, namely, that we exist in a universe that is good, and that we are in it to experience good.

"The earth is the Lord's, and the fulness thereof; the world, and they that dwell therein" (Psalms 24:1). This happens to be so. Make this personal to you in this treatment:

MY PRESENT WORLD, RIGHT HERE AND RIGHT NOW, IS SATURATED WITH A DIVINE INTELLIGENCE, A CREATIVE PURPOSE, A RESPONDING LIFE, FOR THAT WHICH CREATED ME, CREATED ME OUT OF ITSELF. THEREFORE, I AM LIVING THAT LIFE THAT IS THE LIFE OF THE UNIVERSE. I AM LOVING WITH THAT LOVE THAT IS THE LOVE OF THE UNIVERSE. I AM THINKING WITH THAT MIND THAT IS THE MIND OF THE UNIVERSE. "I AND MY FATHER ARE ONE" (John 10:30). "HE THAT SEETH ME SEETH HIM THAT SENT ME" (John 12:45). THESE STATEMENTS ARE TRUE OF MYSELF BECAUSE THEY ARE TRUE OF GOD.

"You Can" is the truth. Some wit has said that the greatest mistake the Divine Mind ever made was to give man free will— because while man *could*, he also *couldn't* if he thought that he couldn't. Man could select the affirmative, the creative, the positive; but he could also select the negative, the destructive and the unhappy. And this is what we have been doing since evolution began. We have free will. We are able to create a good personal life and we are able to create a destructive life, whichever way we decide to chart our course.

Many people say that their negatives are not their fault, that they are the result of conditions that the world has produced around them, or the result of conditions they grew up in, conditions in their family and environment. This is an explanation, but it is not a cure. There is a great difference between an explanation and a cure.

Let us use the illustration that I have a cold, which I don't have. (It is interesting that, since I wrote my booklet on "The Cause and Cure of the Common Cold,"* I have not had any. I bless the typewriter that I typed the booklet on because I apparently finally convinced myself that I would not have another cold, and I haven't.) I could start my explanation of it by saying that I spent last evening in air-conditioning, which does not give you colds; or that I sat near a fan; or that I was riding in a car and all the windows were down. I could give myself the explanation, but I couldn't give myself the cure until I went to work in my own mind and eliminated the emotional confusion and emotional congestion which were the real cause of my cold. No one has ever caught cold from the elements, no one ever will; and I state this flatly and definitely. You develop colds only from emotional congestion and emotional confusion.

* See p. 87.

The explanation is not the cure, even though Sigmund Freud thought that it was. He thought that the explanation produced the cure. Later authorities in his field of psychoanalysis discovered that not always was there a cure from merely the explanation. Rather, a positive factor had to be introduced to bring about the cure.

Whenever you are in a problem, the question is, "What positive factor can I introduce into this problem?" The explanation of the problem will not cure the problem. The explanation of a man who is bankrupt will not get him out of bankruptcy. It will explain how he got in, but it will not tell him how to get out. The person who explains his problems is only explaining how something was brought about, but he is not explaining the cure.

In the book *Reality Therapy*, by Dr. William Glasser, the author, who is a psychiatrist, states very bluntly that the first step toward a cure is decision. When you arrive at a decision, a creative idea can then operate in your mind. He says that there are no emotionally sick people; there are only indecisive people who need to arrive at a decision; and when they arrive at a decision, when they face themselves and decide upon a creative course, these people are always immediately improved and are able, with help, to work their way out of their problems.

When I read this book, it made a tremendous impression on me. It changed a great deal of my own thinking and the way I think when I am counseling with people in trouble. More and more, I am making people arrive at a positive decision because I know that the ideas they need will come to them after they have arrived at a positive conclusion. These ideas cannot arrive as long as they are going around the circle from the beginning symptom to the present trouble, then going back from the present to the beginning, and back again.

New ideas do not happen in a mind that is engrossed in past experience. Creative ideas do not happen to the mind that is engrossed only in the explanation of evil or in the explanation of why an individual is in trouble. They appear when he stops thinking of his trouble and starts thinking of his solution. When the mind is diverted from the negative stream of consciousness to the positive stream of consciousness, then the positive stream of consciousness is able to generate within that person the right creative ideas, the right answers, the right suggestions, the right directions and the right motivations. Once the mind has been switched from the "I Can't" to the "I Can," from the fact that I am in trouble to the creative stimulation that I am going to get out of trouble, the trouble has received its death warrant. Until the attention is shifted, there is very little that the person can do for himself or, may I add, that anyone else can do for him.

Someone remarked to me recently that, even in the business world, when you solve another person's problem, eventually that person comes back with another problem similar to it. You can bring only temporary relief to another's problem. Only when the person arrives at his or her own conclusion to do something about it will he find his answer appearing in his own consciousness.

Paul wrote, "I can do all things through an Indwelling Power." He used a different theological term, but this is what he meant. He said, "I can do all things through Christ which strengtheneth me" (Philippians 4:13). Paul distinguished the difference between Jesus the man, and the Idea which worked through Jesus, by the term *Christ*. Often, when Paul wrote of Jesus, he spoke of him as Christ Jesus, meaning that the spiritual essence was more important than the physical, factual man. "I can do all things through Christ which strengtheneth me," meaning through the Power, the Mind, the Intelligence and the interior Action of God. In your thinking, say it often: "I can do all things through the action of God that strengtheneth me."

We have been told to be self-reliant, and at the same time we have created a gadget world so that we aren't self-reliant. If you have a copy of Emerson's essays, it would be a good thing to read his essay "Self Reliance." Way back then, in the 1840s, this great classic came forth from the pen of Ralph Waldo Emerson. He said, in essence, the same thing that Paul wrote and that other great minds, in both religion and philosophy, have said—that the individual is already equipped to solve his problems.

Unless you are in a totally unconscious state, there is always something creative that you can do. If you have been knocked down by an automobile and are in a hospital, and you are totally unconscious, then you have to have others take care of you until you can think. But unless you are in a totally unconscious state, you can always do something creative to get yourself out of a situation. You are equipped by the nature of life to do this.

When I think of the greatness of the Infinite Spirit, I think of what It did in creating me, my loved ones, my friends, my associates in business. This is a magnificent illustration of what a Great Mind can do. Not only did It create me physically, It created me as a mind-emotion individual. It created me to think and to feel. It created me with free will to decide the issues of my life. It created me with this equipment so that I need not lean on anyone else. I need not always reach out to my world for help. I need not others to create my panacea. I have within myself the equipment necessary to function fully in life.

We are often warped and crippled by errors of the past, if you want to call them that; by situations in which we find ourselves which we may not have created at all but which made great impressions on us. But the past can always be made as nothing when the present becomes the future.

I admit the problems of the past. I grew up as you did, and growing up is not easy. We like, as we grow older, to look back in retrospection and glamorize our childhood. There is no glamour in childhood and in growing up. If you are honest with yourself, you know this. It is very nice to look back and glamorize it, but it was _____. (I was going to use a word that I shouldn't use even though as a clergyman I am licensed to use it. It is about a certain location with fires burning underneath it. I will write it this way and not offend.)

Many people were born in very difficult circumstances and grew up in very difficult environments. However, the past can always be negated when the present becomes the future. Too many of us are only looking at the now, forgetting that tomorrow is being born today. We forget that the next year and the experiences we will have in it are being born right now. The calendar is always old before it unravels its next year. Your next year will be what *you* are *this* year. We always make the future in the present. Realize that any negative condition continues only as long as it is given attention.

The New Testament tells us that people were healed just by looking at Jesus or by touching the hem of his garment. I can understand this. Their attention was diverted from their problems by the tremendous personality of the man. For a split second, they forgot their problems. For a moment, they looked upon an individual whom they considered superior to themselves, and this was enough to produce a dramatic change in these people. They were able to think of a well, strong, vital, creative man and, in so doing, they forgot their own ailments long enough for their healings to take place.

"Look unto me, and be ye saved, all the ends of the earth: for I am God, and there is none else" (Isaiah 44:22). Again, you have the shifting of the attention from the problem to the solution; from the difficulty to the answer. By the shifting of consciousness, we change the events in our lives.

Can this be practical? Of course it is practical. This is the method we use in our entire Science of Mind, which is Religious Science. We are deliberately shifting our attention over to the "I Can" side of life. I can do it. There is That within me which can do it. I do not need to rely only on my own intellectual understanding of life. There is the Power of God resident in my soul which gives me the right idea so that I can accomplish everything that I want to accomplish. The idea I need does not come to me as a rush of emotion or through any implausible action. It comes to me as a great creative idea. It happens in my mind because it is already there, ready to happen when I have opened the door of my own thought and made it possible for it to appear. It is already within me.

The old adage that there is nothing new under the sun is absolutely correct. Any idea that ever will be, already is. It may not have appeared in someone's mind as yet, but it will. Every idea is already in the Universal Mind, the Mind of God, and this Mind is your mind, this Mind is my mind. There are not two minds; there is one Mind operating through all people, just as there is one Life, one Love, one of anything.

There is one set of numbers. When you say one, two, three, and on to nine, you are using the same set of numbers Einstein used. You are using the same numbers that the greatest mathematical physicists in the world are using. They are not your numbers, yet they are yours to use. Whenever you use these in any combination, you are using a common denominator of mathematics. You use them your way and Einstein used them his way. The great men of science today are using those same numbers; they are no different. Their numbers are not gold-plated against yours being nickel. They are the same numbers, the same value, same everything, because there is only one set of numbers—one, two, three, and so on. The entire field of mathematics is nothing but a combination of these numbers, the use of these numbers, and you have these numbers. There is one set of numbers, and you use them.

There is one alphabet, and you use it. Everyone uses the same alphabet. The alphabet I am using is the alphabet you use. We are using the same alphabet, the same system of numbers, the same air, the same water, etc.

There is one common denominator of numbers; there is one common denominator of the alphabet in the English language. There is one common denominator back of all life. There is one God, one Mind, one Spirit, one Truth, one Intelligence, one Law of Its Action, one Way in which It works. You and I are always in It, of It and are It, and we are using It. To some, it seems wrong to say that we are using God. I am using air in order to breathe, in order to write this. I am using ideas that come through my mind as I am writing. All of this to me is Life. I am not worried about using anything. The only thing I am worried about is the people who don't use what they have.

You are equipped with an "I Can" process. It is the same "I Can" process that you find in all successful people. You say, "If only I had what this person has," and you will name it. "If only I had that." But you already have it. There is nothing in any Head of State that you do not have in your consciousness. There is nothing in the great wisdom of the ages that you do not have. We are all in the same Intelligence; we are all in the same Wisdom; and we are all in the same Mind.

When you see this, you may be a failure but, if you are, you do not blame it on the universe. You may be chronically ill, but you cannot blame it on the universe. Somewhere along the line you did not use the success equipment you have in order to prevent this situation. Always there is a prevention when you shift your attention to make the present the future. When you do that, you move from the "I Can't" to the "I Can." I cease my condemnation of the world for making me sick, miserable, unhappy, poor and afraid because it hasn't done this. I cease my condemnation of other people and I am set free to be what I now decide I shall be. There is a Power at the center of me, which Paul called the Christ, the Old Testament called the I Am. Jesus called It the Father, and today, in the field of modern metaphysics, we call It the Indwelling Mind. I can do all things because of the spiritual equipment which is already in my mind. It is already there, waiting to act, waiting to become, when I make my demand upon It. I make my demand upon It by saying that It is so.

The prophet Joel wrote, "Let the weak say, I am strong" (Joel 3:10), meaning let these people change their minds. Instead of the recitation of what they can't do, start them on a recitation of what they can do.

People often come to me with their problems and say, "Everything has gone wrong in my world." I mentally reverse that instantly and say that it is not so. They look at me and start telling me their troubles. After a few minutes, I ask, "What is right in your world? There is something in your world that is right." If they can't think of anything, I say, "At least you have a good complexion." I will say anything to break the circle of recitation of evil; anything to move them from the "I Can't" to the "I Can" level; anything that is constructive, moral and creative to lift them from the level of "Poor Me" to the level of "I Can." I work to lift them from the level of self-depreciation to the level of self-appreciation. This is the only way of thinking if you want to live creatively. If you don't want to live creatively, then this isn't your Teaching.

You were not born to start at the age of six months and go through to the age of ninety with one heartache, headache, and tragedy after another. You have friends who are always bearing up and going through a serious problem and, at the same time, getting ready for the next. They say, "This is the way life is." This is not the way life is. Or they say, "What can you do when the whole world's attention is on war?" I don't believe everybody's attention is on war. If you go to lunch today and they put the menu in front of you, your attention won't be on war; it will be on the menu.

It is easy to slip into the slough of despond without knowing it and to live destructively. Yet at the intellectual level you are saying, "Yes, I know Right Action is so, but I can't make it work for me." If you are one of these people, it is because you have not yet arrived at a decision to change your life. You are still at the "I Can't" level.

Some say, "I don't know enough." The people who have changed the world did not change the world on the basis of what they knew. They changed the world through new ideas which came to them as they acted. They decided to do it. This can also be true of you.

"I don't know enough" is no longer an excuse. The only excuse you can give is, "I really don't want to. I want to stay in my problem. It is comfortable. It gives me a chance to be a martyr. Everyone thinks I am brave, and I like it." I have a healthy respect for such people because they have decided what they are going to do. They have made their decision. Those of us who can't make that kind of decision are in a different spot.

We can change, but it is not dependent on what we know; it is not dependent on past experience; it is not dependent on either our blood line or the environment in which we were raised. It is dependent on our decision to say, "I Can," not "I Will." We say "I Will" so often when we don't mean it. Say, "I can meet any situation that is now a difficulty in my life. I shall continue to meet every situation that appears in my life for as long as I am on this planet. I Can." Further, "I can because I am already equipped to do this. I do not need to get a spiritual unfoldment. I am Spirit unfolding. I do not need to do this, that or the other. I am this, that or the other. My tomorrow is my today. My next year is my this year. That which shall be, already is." Gaze upon that which shall be with the "I Can" attitude and move toward it. You are moving toward your demonstration.

"Look unto me, and be ye saved, all the ends of the earth; for I am God, and there is none else." All the ends of my earth, my home, my office, my career, my loved ones, my social relationships, my income and disbursements—these are the ends of my earth. These are the things which I need to draw together into a single, central focus. If there is nothing besides God, then I am in God, and of God. This is a great statement of monotheism, "For I am God, and there is none else." We are in It. We are of It. It is in action in us.

Convince yourself that you are spiritually equipped to meet every situation; that the Mind of God is your mind right now; that right ideas do prevail; and that whatever needs to be done, you can do it. You can do it in an effortless way. You do not need to be drained of energy. You only need to know that the right idea is always delivered into your mind at the instant that you need it. It is there. It appears. You know it. You think it. You act as it. And it brings forth a result that is creative, that is valuable. It has made you a better person and made your friends and loved ones better people because of the action that has taken place through you. With Paul say, "I can do all things through Christ which strengtheneth me" (Philippians 4:13). Four of the greatest spiritual words ever used in the history of the race are *God Is—I Can.*

The Power that created you is the Power that works through you. The Intelligence which created you out of Itself indwells you. You have the equipment to live life. You have the ability to change your mind. You have the ability to shift your attention. With these keys you are free to do with your life what you select to do. You can remain in the depression, the endless circle of "why." Or you can say that this is unimportant. This is what you intend to do. The great question "Why did it happen to me?" has no answer.

As a student of this Teaching, you don't work with the "why"; you work with the "how." Within you is the Spiritual Equipment which says, "I Can, once I have made my decision."

---

I BELIEVE IN GOD, THE GOOD OMNIPOTENT. I BELIEVE IN THE LIVING SPIRIT OF THE INFINITE MIND AND THE INFINITE LOVE. I BELIEVE IN MYSELF, FOR THAT WHICH CREATED ME, DWELLS IN ME, ACTS THROUGH ME, AND IS THAT WHICH I AM. HERE IS MY SECURITY. HERE IS MY PEACE. TO EVERY SITUATION IN MY WORLD, I SAY, "I CAN." AMEN.

# Love Is Not Enough

*Love is the capacity to give emotion to others and yet neither dominate them nor be dominated by them.*

WE HAVE HAD preachers and others who have believed themselves to be sincere in their faith, who have prattled about love ever since time began—or at least since Christianity began. Love is not emphasized so much in the Old Testament as it is in the New Testament, and that may have been a point of wisdom. But all along the line countless numbers of people have stoutly declared, "Love conquers all."

Well, does it?

One of my responsibilities as a clergyman is to perform wedding ceremonies. I held a beautiful wedding service in our chapel yesterday, and I have another beautiful one to perform today. These young people who are looking forward to a happy marriage are delightful people. You can tell that they are earnest. You can tell that they are honest. You can tell that they really love one another. But the question is, "Will they use wisdom in their love relationship?"

If love in marriage were always balanced with wisdom, we would cut the divorce rate in this country by eighty percent. That would be tremendous, because as you undoubtedly know, there are some places in this country where the divorce rate is higher than the marriage rate.

My aim here is not to offer a treatise on love, marriage and divorce. I am happy for you who are in love. I do not condemn those of you who are divorced. My purpose here is to discuss love in its broadest aspects and various forms, for *love is a widely diversified emotion; an emotion that, in one way or another, is—or should be—experienced by every member of the human race.*

In the beginning, however, I want to dispel the belief that has been, and unfortunately sometimes still is, handed down from many pulpits. This is that Divine Love will do everything— that if we only love God, everything will be all right. I know several people who love God but who cannot get along with people.

Emotion without intelligence cannot function wisely. Love is an emotion. Love and hate are two ends of the same stick, and they cannot function without a balancing of intelligence. Dr. Ernest Holmes, who started this idea called Religious Science, often used to quote a very short statement of Browning's: *All is love, yet all is law.* That statement is quoted in the *Science of Mind* textbook.*

* *The Science of Mind*, by Ernest Holmes, pp. 469, 501.

Many factors are involved in this emotion. It takes wisdom to maintain love. It takes intelligence to maintain love. It takes insight to maintain love. You and I know it. So the statement that God is love is not enough. I do not mean that the statement is incorrect. *God is love, but God is also mind.* God is also a perpetual creative process so that, because of the Divine Intelligence in which we are all immersed, something is being born in every person at every instant, and something is dying in every person at every instant. It is a process of constant flow—a perpetual input and outgo. This process is taking place in all right minds. It is a balance. It is a harmony. It is not an exaggeration on the side of either feeling or intellect.

You know, of course, that you can become so intellectual that you lose most of your capacity to love. You can also get so busy that you lose the capacity to love, or at least it is dormant. The capacity to love then goes beneath the surface, awaiting your recognition. You know people and I know people who are in that position right now. They are doing everything they can to not face the fact that mankind is a unity—that it actually is a brotherhood, and according to today's thinking we must also say sisterhood. You and I are emotionally linked to people one way or another, whether we like it or not. We always have been and we always will be.

The moment that love becomes a duty, it is no longer love. The moment that love is accepted and not promoted, it loses its significance. For two people to love one another, or for a group to love one another—even a group such as we have in our Science of Mind organization, where we have a common idea that we all love—it takes a bit of doing to keep everyone happy. It takes a bit of doing to balance the emotional with the intellectual. It takes a bit of doing because emotions usually govern. In the average person the emotions govern; and when emotions govern, they often go off in wrong directions.

You know that this is true, if you will review your life. I know it, if I will review mine. Does that mean that you and I should conquer our emotions? First of all, we can't do it. And secondly, if we could, we would be of no value to life. We would become mere machines, perhaps not even that. It is certain that we do not want to bottle up our emotions.

The whole field of modern psychology shows that emotions have to be handled or they will handle you. The conclusion that unless you handle your emotion, your emotion handles you is one that has received great emphasis ever since the discoveries made by Sigmund Freud. We are all aware of certain people who are emotionally run, and we are aware of people who are run strictly by their intellect. Both sets of individuals are tragic people. Again I ask the question, "Is love enough?" Again the answer is "No."

Some of my old-time adherents are going to say, "But, Dr. Barker, you wrote about the idea that loving God was all that was necessary many years ago." I know. There was a time when I *Divine-Loved* everything. But as I matured, I began to develop a wiser view.

People often say to me now, "Jesus loved everybody." He did not. Read the Book again. He hated the Pharisees. He couldn't stand the Sadducees. He said so very definitely, very specifically. So Jesus didn't love everybody. Read the books. They are four little books called the four Gospels. Then read the three wonderful Epistles of John on love. They are glorious. It will take you all of fifteen minutes to read them. After you have read them, say to yourself, "What did he really mean?"

At this point some readers are likely to think that I am a cynic; that I am ruling out love. Not at all. I am not cynical about love. I know from my own life what it has done. I know what the support and greatness of love has meant in my experience. However, I am cynical about using love as an overall formula for the solution of all problems. For instance, we didn't get those astronauts up in orbit with love, even though they came from happy families. We got them up there because of an action of Mind in the minds of many, many scientists and laymen. Divine Love didn't put the men on the moon, though the men on the moon had this love within them at the time they were on the moon. They took it with them and they brought it back, because everyone is born of the Spirit. Everyone is born of Love, but everyone also is born of Mind. Of course, love is still the great emotion.

How can we define it? Nearly all psychologists have tried to do this, and they have come up with innumerable definitions. Let's put it this way: *Love is a creative emotion induced by relationships with people and maintained in balance.* It is the main, essential emotion of life, and it is creative. It is not dormant. It is an improving emotion when it is experienced. However, I know people who are nicer to their dogs than they are to their neighbors. I am delighted that they love their dogs. Loving a pet is a wonderful outlet for creative emotion.

To repeat, love is a creative emotion which has to be in relationship to others—or to the dog or the cat—which is maintained with wisdom. Even the dog has to be disciplined, and even you and I as adults have to be disciplined. If we do not discipline ourselves, then life does it for us. Life invites us to grow but it cannot compel. It can impel but it cannot compel, because you and I have free will. I am free to hate. I am free to criticize. I am free to condemn. I am also free to praise. I am also free to tell people that they are wonderful. A great many people in your world and mine are wonderful. But many individuals never think to tell others that. They just go along, hit-and-miss. Then, when they get into a real problem, they may say *I love you* to someone who is helpful. But do they really mean it?

Here, in the broad field of love, is power—a depth of psychological power. It is a power that man has struggled to understand. He has struggled to find out what this thing is that he feels that is beyond definition. Why is it that he loves a certain person? Why does he love his family or a platonic friend? Why is it that he loves a certain hobby? Look at the men and women who love fishing. There is nothing wrong with that. At least it gives them some peace and quiet. Look at the thousands today who love skiing. They are emotionally bound to skiing.

You have your things to which you are bound by love, and I have mine. Everyone else loves someone or something when there is a healthy emotional release. If there is not, those emotional bonds can hurt and become unhealthy. That is why love has to be balanced with wisdom. That is why you must watch your emotions; they are the most powerful directive forces of your life. Many of you will say, "But I was taught in the old days of my Religious Science experience that I must watch my thoughts." Thoughts are secondary to emotions. Thoughts can direct emotions, but thought is secondary to feeling. Feeling is the most important function of life, especially in personal relationships.

In the flow of people into your office or mine; in the flow of people in your social life or mine; with the people in your home, family and associations, your feelings play a paramount role. Those whom you love, or with whom you are closely associated, know when you are disturbed without your saying a word. You know when they are disturbed without their saying a word. This is because love responds to love, just as mind responds to mind. As idea responds to idea, so emotion responds to emotion. Here is the field of first cause. Here is the germinating field in which ideas can be born. Here is the womb of creation.

We know that feeling is an emotion, but where is feeling? Feeling is in your subconscious mind. You cannot *cause* love with your intellect. Sometimes you and I watch people try to do it. They have picked out a person, or a group, and intellectually they see that person or group as exactly what they would like to belong to. But they can't blend with the person or persons they have selected. They try, and they try hard. Why don't they succeed? Because their emotions say *no*. This explains why mothers love their wayward children more then they do those who are perfect. Mothers always seem to love the boy or girl who runs away, gets into trouble and comes back. I think that is great. At least the child knows he or she can come back.

It is our emotions that take us where we are going. If you can, in quietness, sometime make a list of the people, the things, the hobbies and the pursuits that you love, you will have a map of your constructive emotions. Then make a list of the things you can't stand, can't abide and really hate. You will have a second blueprint of emotions—this time, of your destructive emotions. You may not like what you see, but at least you will be seeing it.

Many people ask me, "Can I develop the capacity to love?" Of course you can. Like any other quality of life, you can develop it. How do you do it? You do it by saying that you are love's embodiment. That's all. Simply say, "I AM LOVE." I can just see some of the businessmen's heads shaking. But that is a good statement to repeat once in a while. Your subconscious mind knows that you are brilliant, intellectually. It knows you are a good businessman or a good businesswoman. But every once in a while say: "Wait a minute. I am fundamentally feeling. *How* am I feeling?"

Coming back to my wedding services: when I perform them I do not say *unto death do us part*, because that puts a dread finality on the union. The marriage may or may not work in today's society. So I leave that statement out. Years ago I left out the word "duty." You cannot prophesy the success or the failure of a marriage. You cannot prophesy love. You can hope, and you can plan for it. You can intelligently direct it, and you probably can prolong it as long as you are around, but it takes a bit of doing. Too often when a person falls madly in love—be it a young person or a frisky senior citizen—he or she just throws intelligence out the door, throws wisdom out the window. Your love for a person must be tempered with wisdom, and so must your love for an animal, love for a member of your family or love for your business.

I happen to love my business, but I have to watch it. I can overly intellectualize it. Watch how you are using your basic emotion. You don't always call it love. You can use any number of names, and you can love greatly without ever saying so. But then you are robbing yourself of a great deal of self-expression, and you are not letting other people know that you can love.

I watch people frequently—on the street, in a restaurant, or on a bus or subway. Sometimes I just watch and say, "I wonder if that man or that woman loves someone." I don't know who they are, and of course I don't get an answer. After musing for a while, I say to myself, "What about my own love? I had better express it in a more balanced way." What we all need is Divine Mind and Divine Love, not Divine Love and Divine Mind. We need intellect balanced with emotion, not emotion balanced with intellect.

When your emotion and intellect are balanced, I believe you can talk about love spiritually. I don't think love is spiritual unless it is balanced with intelligence. Does that mean that if you love a situation, a person or a condition you will intellectualize yourself out of it? No. It merely means that you must be on the watch for any imbalance. Love is spiritual only when it is creative, and it is creative only when it is intelligent.

You may know some strange people who have married other

strange people, according to your way of looking at it. Yet they seem to get along fine. They do so because they are making a job of it. One is not possessing the other. One is not demanding too much from the other. One is not emotionally imprisoning the other. There is a wonderful interplay which makes this marriage work. It isn't just the beautiful people who can know love. The movies would like you to think so, and other businesses advertising the virtue of youth would like you to think so.

Love has no age level. It knows no beginning and no end. When you touch love it doesn't know your age, and it isn't interested; just as when you touch intelligence, it doesn't know your age and it isn't interested. The great, great values of life know you only as their potential outlet, and that's all they are interested in.

It is easy to go back twenty years, to think about the love you experienced in those days and see where you made some mistakes or where you experienced a definite victory. But that's no longer important. Here you are *right now*, and here you are equipped with both emotion and intelligence. So what do you do from here?

You will remember one of my pet expressions as I relate this story. I gave it to a man who had just come out of the hospital after having undergone a very serious operation. He was preparing to leave for another part of the country. When he came into my office he did what they always do. He immediately went over all of the gory details from the time he had entered the hospital until the time he left. In fact the miserable circumstances continued until he got to my office, because he had had great difficulty in getting a taxi. When he finished his tale of woe, I said, "Okay. You are going back to another state—across the country. Are you going to take that hospital with you, and the surgeon, and the nurses, and the food, and the pain and medication? Is that what is getting into the plane with you tomorrow? Is that what is in your baggage? Because you can linger in those halls of memory for a long, long time."

He asked me what I would do, and I said I didn't know. Perhaps I would do the same thing he was doing. "But," I told him, "I have a phrase that I want you to memorize. It is this: *Yesterday ended last night.*"

He looked at me and asked me not to say another word. He took time out to think and then declared: "When I get on that plane at noon tomorrow I will have my baggage and my clothes, but I am leaving that hospital in New York; and I am leaving that wonderful, wise surgeon in New York. I am leaving those wonderful nurses in New York, too. That's where they are doing their perfect work to help people. I am not going to take them with me. *Yesterday ended last night.*"

You could see his shoulders relax. You could imagine that, living in California as he does with all of his friends, he could repeat this recital for days, even months. But he left all of the hospital experience behind him. It is so easy to keep the past in the present when it is destructive. And the emotions enjoy this replay of negatives. This man could have gotten a kick out of telling the hospital story, but he is a very sincere student of our beliefs and he had the strength to promise to forego that pleasure.

What are you going to do with your emotions? Are you going to hang on to the old destructive ones or are you going to develop a new viewpoint? Do you believe you should love everyone? I don't. I have quite a list of people I don't care about. That doesn't mean that I hate them. It just means that I couldn't care less. I am trying somewhat to overcome the feeling of disinterest. We all should acknowledge that life is spiritual, creative, loving and wise. This is the unity and this is the oneness that philosophers have discussed in the past and are discussing now. This is the cosmic order; this is the whole world. It is the one-family concept we always have had as an ideal, and it has to remain an ideal until we evolve further. We know that it is *possible*, even if it is not *probable*. So let us work toward that end, because we have to work toward that which the world says can't be, but which we as spiritual beings know can be. Not all doors are shut; not all avenues are closed. As a creative mind with creative emotions, you are the hope of the world; as a noncreative person with negative emotions, you are deterring the advance of all of society. You have free will, of course, and can choose to be either creative or noncreative.

Some of you will tell me that you have been unhappy all these years. Can you be happy? Paul, in his writings, says it can happen in the twinkling of an eye. However, I think it takes hard work; but it can be done. As I said before, we of Religious Science are the people who say, ''I was created by an infinite wisdom, intelligence, love and balance. I am not going to believe in things that can't be done, because I am too busy working on the things that can be.'' There is not one of you who read this who couldn't love more.

The wise men and women of the East and the West have said that the universe is a unity; it is a *one thing*. Pythagoras said all numbers are one. There is only one number, *number one*. All others are branches from it. Great mystics say that we are one brotherhood of people. Intuitively we know that this is so. Even though on the surface our world may look like a cracked egg, underneath it all there is a wholeness. Let's do some right thinking about it. We can all make our contribution of *more love balanced with wisdom*, for, after all, love alone is not enough.

# How to Change Other People

*Sometimes people take out on others the things they don't solve for themselves.*

METAPHYSICS IS THE SCIENCE of handling our own thought, not the handling of other people's thought. Yet one of the commonest problems brought to the offices and classrooms of every spiritual teacher and practitioner is the question of how we can pray scientifically and thus treat the other person in order to make him into the type of character we want him to be according to our own standards. If any Truth teachers were to lower their standards and present a method of erroneous treatment for the changing of other people, they would undoubtedly draw tremendous audiences; but no teacher worthy of the Christ message would do so.

66

Personal relationships are one of the major problems of all people. They always have been and they will continue to be until the masses of people assimilate the teachings of Jesus as an instruction in the handling of states of consciousness and not continue in the vain attempt to manipulate personalities at will. Most people when confronted with a difficult person forget that superb biblical phrase "Look unto me and be ye saved" (Isaiah 45:22), and in its place they unconsciously use the incorrect thought "Look unto me and be ye hurt and confused."

Then how is this problem to be met, and what instruction can we give to the earnest people asking this question? Most of us labor under the delusion that we are constantly in contact with "difficult people." We see them as needing so much correcting, and in so doing we fail to realize that we are actually stating our own insufficiencies in the handling of our own mental responses to these same people. "Like attracts like," and this Law of Mind-action cautions us that if the people we contact are unpleasant, then there must be a premise for that unpleasantness within ourselves.

While it is true that we are living in a material world and should not deny it, nevertheless that which makes the material world important to the individual is not the world itself, but the states of consciousness induced in the person as he mentally responds to his world. For example, wherever you are as you read this booklet look around you. You are apparently surrounded by material walls, objects and people. However, the only way that you know this is that your five senses are reporting these facts to your brain centers, and they in turn cause your consciousness to be conditioned with certain mental responses. So you say to yourself that you are at such-and-such a place, certain definite material things are around you, certain activities are taking place and certain people are present. Actually, you are merely defining your mental and emotional responses to the stimuli brought to your attention by means of the five senses. An intoxicated person in the same spot you are now occupying would get an entirely different mental response from the same scene. A blind person would get another, and a deaf person still another. Each would interpret his material world at the level of his unconscious mental response to the stimuli presented to him as a result of his immediate environment.

Thus you actually do not live in a material world. You live in a realm of consciousness generated by your own mental reactions to the world, and these have arrived at the threshold of your awareness by means of your five senses. To these impressions flowing to you from the outside world is added your subconscious accumulation of thought patterns which also condition your responses, and the sum total is your present state of awareness or consciousness. When you go to sleep at night you may dream of many places, objects and people. Your dream reaction is as real at the instant it takes place as your material-world reaction is when you are awake. In the dream state you are experiencing definite mental responses, but in this case the stimuli for them are brought to the surface of your mind from subconscious thought forms. But it is just as real to you at the time you are dreaming it.

In other words, your individual world, whether asleep or awake, is to you what your consciousness reports it to be. This is an important point and one which if properly assimilated will cause you to revalue your world and see it from a viewpoint that is right. When Jesus said, "I am not of this world" (John 8:23), he meant the material world of fact and form as the average person believes it to be. Jesus knew that his world was one of his own consciousness, and there he maintained the sort of mental responses he wanted to experience. Thus the material world of his day could persecute him, but because of his controlled thinking, such evil never confounded him, for he viewed it correctly and handled his thought about it perfectly. Jesus could see God everywhere and in all people, because he had only God in his thought, and thus he responded only to God's presence.

Once you have accepted the foregoing ideas as truth, then you can go forward another step in your thinking about how to change other people. Not only is your opinion of the world around you the result of your mental reaction to it, but also the people in your world are to you what you mentally conceive them to be as a result of your mental responses to them. A great many of the readers of this booklet work all week in an office or some other place of business. In such a place there is usually some other employee who annoys you greatly. You could mentally wring his neck with great joy. Every time you come into contact with him you receive a negative reaction. He annoys you, possibly even angers you, and you usually think that if only that one party would resign and go somewhere else, your world would automatically be happier and more efficient.

However, you are still dealing only with your mental response to that person, as we have just seen. You go home after your day's work and you tell a member of your family all about this problem-child of yours. You can describe with great detail the petty annoyances he has caused you. Your description is vivid and definite. But what are you describing? This difficult person is not in your home at that hour; probably he is many miles away; so you are describing only your own mental picture of him. You are portraying one of your own states of consciousness. You are giving evidence of your own wrong thinking yet blaming the other party for it. No one is the thinker within you but yourself. If you are thinking and speaking negatively about someone, that person is not to blame for your mental response to him. You are the only thinker in your universe.

The next morning you sit down to breakfast in your own home. Everything is peaceful, and order prevails. The food is good, and if there is another with you, you chat amiably. There isn't a thing in the room to annoy you or upset you. If you are still disturbed in your thought over this person from the previous day, it is because you are still carrying a wrong thought pattern of him in your consciousness. You have no right to bring such a mental attitude to your breakfast table, for even as your body will assimilate the food that you eat, so will your consciousness for the day absorb the negation you are maintaining. The walls around you are not interested in your hurt feelings. The table and food before you do not care about your state of mind. They are merely fulfilling the purpose for which they were created. You, and you alone, are the burden-bearer of vicious thinking.

At this point most people start reciting all their reasons as to why they should carry forward their hurt viewpoint. They use excuse after excuse to justify their wrong thinking. Their reasoning seems to them to be valid, and they say that if only they could get their hands on that person they would tell him just what they think about him, etc. This is the devil in action; this is evil attempting to make itself real. There is not a word of Truth in the entire description. True, when they meet him later in the day the old vicious thinking may start all over again, but at that breakfast table there is no justification for holding on to an ugly mental state that should have been forgiven and forgotten twelve to sixteen hours before.

I am certain that this is what Jesus meant when he said, "Forgive, if ye have ought against any" (Mark 11:25). To do this is not difficult. You stand in need of treatment; and treatment is a mental process by which you delete from your consciousness the negative reactions and in their place establish the positives. You need only to sit down quietly and do your mental work in this way:

*God as Infinite Mind is now here, and I am a thinking*
*center in this One Mind. I refuse to have what I believe*
*is an unpleasant person ruin my consciousness today.*
*I say to my false responses to this person, as Jesus said*
*to Peter, "Get thee behind me Satan; thou art an offence*
*unto me, for thou savourest not the things that be of*
*God" (Matthew 16:23). I refuse to think that John or*
*Mary is a vicious and difficult person. I care not what*
*evidences my five senses bring to me as supposed facts.*
*I now only know that John or Mary is a spiritual being,*
*the perfect creation of a Perfect Mind. I behold him as*
*God beholds him—honest, loving and cooperative.*

Then go forth to your day and stand watch over your
thought. Each time the old reaction appears, stop it at once in
your own thought and declare silently, "This is not true of God,
therefore it is not true of this person. I behold only God in action, here and now in this friend." Gradually the change will
take place, and as the universe responds through corresponding, this person in your world will no longer continue to annoy
you. Rather, he will become a co-worker with you and a friend
along the way.

The only thing that ever needs to be conditioned or recon-
ditioned is your own mentality. One of the major characteristics of our metaphysical teaching that differentiate us from the
older religious bodies is that our work is one of individual information, not individual reformation. Jesus did not reform anyone. He told men the Truth, and as they absorbed it they were
transformed by the renewing of their minds. When you have
been informed that you are the only thinker in your universe,
and therefore the only thing that needs to be corrected is your
own state of consciousness, then you can change your reactions

to anyone in the world, because you will know how to control your mental responses. People, like things, are to us what we mentally conceive them to be. Most people are hungering and thirsting for someone who loves them enough to overlook their human frailties and behold the action of God within them. Look around you, and with Paul of Tarsus declare: "Christ in you, the hope of glory" (Colossians 1:27).

"And why beholdest thou the mote that is in thy brother's eye, but considerest not the beam that is in thine own eye?" In these words from the Sermon on the Mount you have a frank statement of the idea necessary for changing other people.

There is not a word in the Bible that says you have to put up with difficult people. In fact, on almost every page there is clear instruction on the necessity of right thinking about other people. Too often you live or work with people for many years and gradually your negative attitude about them warps your whole body of consciousness until you become embittered and defeated. You have the mistaken belief that "this is my cross to bear." Remember that Jesus bore his cross only a little more than three hours. Three hours is long enough for anyone to indulge in evil about their fellowman. Rise up in the integrity of your own Spiritual Nature and command the actions of your mentality as you would the actions of anyone employed by you. Treat and pray until your thought is clear, your speech is positive and you walk free from all error into the way of Truth. Then the correction will have been made in the only place that the great illumined minds have taught as being real, the place of your own inner self.

The only method that Jesus ever used to change other people was to see them as divine in his own thought of them. When people came to him to be healed, they were healed by something which he did inwardly and mentally. He and the patient needing help were in the One Mind, and his silent treatment changed a habit pattern in the patient's subconscious, whereupon the body healing was an automatic reaction to that change. Never do we find him condemning those who were ill. Not a word of criticism fell from his lips. He merely knew within himself that all that was needed was a clarification of his own concept of them, and the perfect Law of Cause and Effect then produced the healing.

Jesus standing before Pilate silent and strong is the greatest proof of this instruction. He could so easily have refuted the false charges, the incriminating statements and the subtle insinuations. But self-justification was never his way. He stood in the knowledge of an immortal security which comes not from adjustment to the world but from a detachment from the world through right understanding of its processes. No man could hurt Jesus. He carried no false mental pictures in his consciousness to make him vulnerable to being hurt. Not even Judas or Pilate had been able to register a mental response in him other than good. He knew only that they were misguided and deluded people who knew not what they really did but couldn't help doing it, for that was their way of looking at their world. There was no one to blame. There were no mistakes made. There were only two differing viewpoints which could not blend together. So the material viewpoint thought it was winning by nailing a man to a cross; but the right-thinking viewpoint of Jesus was the victor after all.

Jesus standing silent before Pilate was treating Pilate. He was knowing that God in this man was the only real Truth of the man. As a result of this mental work, Pilate brings him forth to the multitude and says, "Behold your King" (John 19:14); but again the material viewpoint intervenes, and the world thought says, "Away with him." Many a person has found himself on trial in the situations and personalities of his own everyday life, and too often his consciousness has been crowded with the thoughts of self-righteousness, moral proofs and alibis. Whenever this has happened, the human consciousness again says, "Away with him," and that person is headed for trouble. Watch over the thoughts of your mind and never let the rabble of your own wrong viewpoints crucify you, for they will always try to do this. "What I say unto you I say unto all, Watch" (Mark 13:37).

The Metaphysical Movement of America is seeking to bring together a great mass of people who are willing to handle their own thought. We are not out to change the world, for God made it, and His Mind will direct it into paths of peace and prosperity when we learn to live in it wisely. What other religious bodies do is none of our business, except as we bless and appreciate them. We desire to live in a Divinely ordered universe filled with loving and cooperative people. We turn often to our Bible and find that it reassures us that we can do just that, if we change ourselves into the people God intended us to be. Part of this process is to love our enemies and do good to them that persecute us. This can only be accomplished through an understanding that our consciousness, and it alone, needs correction.

When next you would complain of others, remember that "Silence is Golden," and in the silence of your own thought join with the great Teacher of tones of thought and moods of feeling and walk his way with him. His was the controlled mind, and in that consciousness there were no negative responses. Remember that you are the only thinker within your consciousness, and the Law of Mind produces what you think. Your fellowman is the incarnation of God, whether he knows it or not, whether he acts like it or not. All that Infinite Spirit requires of you is to be faithful unto that which God is in you and to behold God in your fellowman.

*Judge not, that ye not be judged. For with what judgment ye judge, ye shall be judged; and with what measure ye mete, it shall be measured to you again.*

*And why beholdest thou the mote that is in thy brother's eye, but considerest not the beam that is in thine own eye?*

*Or how wilt thou say to thy brother, Let me pull out the mote out of thine eye; and, behold, a beam is in thine own eye?*

Matthew 7:1–4

> The only method that Jesus ever used to Change Other People was to correct his own thought.

# The Science of Forgiveness

*There is no such thing as an evil person, but only a person using life tragically.*

THERE HAVE BEEN many people in your experience whom you did not want to forgive. They were nasty people. They were mean people. But you realized that the lack of forgiveness on your part did them no harm at all, and you also realized that it did hurt you—so you forgave them; not because you were holy; not even because the Bible told you to do so. You forgave them because your own sense of personal security and your desire to live effectively told you that you should do it if you were to be successful. Forgiveness is spiritual life insurance.

We cannot afford to live with a hate. We are living in a world which has more hate in it today than it has ever had before, because there is more conscious intelligence. Each time we expand education we do not develop greater peace or greater love. Every report of increased millions of educated people in the world is accompanied by newspaper headlines of ever-increasing difficulties. We value education, but we realize that education is not the panacea of the world. With an ever-increasing educational program in every country, we have at the same time an ever-increasing group dislike.

Perhaps we are more impressed by our difficulties than were our great-grandfathers, as they did not have accurate information available in their newspapers or at the turn of the dial on a radio. Their worlds consisted mainly of the country in which they lived and the immediate area surrounding it. Today we need to watch our thought more carefully than they did, because we are being bombarded on every side with negatives. I doubt if an atomic war could do as much damage physically as the perpetual bombardment of negatives is already doing spiritually and mentally. We should be alert to the fact that ideas are the most potent force in the world and that states of mind—not people, and not situations—change history.

Jesus did not change history. Jesus engendered an idea in the race mind which changed history. Charles Fillmore once remarked that Jesus' teaching was a blood transfusion for the entire race. It put new life into a worn-out system. It brought something fresh, pure and clean into a world that sorely needed it. We are in such a world today. We are being bombarded by racial, political, national, and even hemispheric hatreds. Enter any gathering of people, and within ten minutes you will discover whom they do not like; but it may take two hours to discover whom they do like.

If you are surrounded by an atmosphere that is distinctly negative, what can you do about it? Any situation of which you are aware, you can handle. If a fire starts in a partition of a building, and it smoulders for hours, no one can do anything about it until either the smoke or the flames make themselves obvious. When you are aware of evil, you can correct it.

We know everything we need to know at this instant to live life wisely. Yet the world opinion comes in and sways us. We are swept into generalities without thinking them through. We tend to accept these generalities because we are used to them, because they are traditional, or because they are seemingly respectable. We do not realize that we are adding fire to the problem by our passive acceptance of it.

What has this to do with the subject of forgiveness? All forgiveness is really self-forgiveness. Your world is the result of your combined state of thought and feeling—your area of consciousness. If your world is the result of your state of consciousness, then if you hate anyone, you are disliking a part of yourself.

You always see your consciousness in your world. Let your fellowman do what he wants to do. Let him say what he wants to say. Let him be as unpleasant as he wants to be; it is none of your business. Even when his reactions affect you, it is still none of your business. You look out at your world through the atmosphere of your thought. "The thing you are looking for is the thing you are looking with, and the thing you are looking at" (Ernest Holmes). If there are people in your world whom you dislike, they are in your world because they are a part of your consciousness. Within your consciousness you are carrying these people, and your own wrong thought is to blame.

The premise for healing a situation through metaphysics is: first, logic and reason; second, treatment. Your logic and reason tell you that these people are not now present. Your logic and reason tell you that there is no reason why you should be upset and conditioned by something which happened in the past. Jesus said, "Let the dead bury the dead," meaning let old situations go—they are not important. Your grudges, your dislikes and your animosities do nothing to the other person, but they wreck you.

It is good spiritual life insurance not to carry grudges. We do not believe we should be sweet to everyone who is unpleasant. We do not teach people to "grin and bear it." We teach people to face facts.

The reason that the ideas of Jesus can change your world is that he met situations the way you would like to meet them. He was able to do things that you wish you could do. You, also, would like to quietly say to your problems, "To this end was I born. For this cause came I into the world." Pilate did not bother Jesus, for Jesus knew that he could not afford to let Pilate confuse him. Jesus knew that the moment he hated Pilate, the High Priest, or Judas, he would never leave the cross, nor come out of the tomb. These men arrayed themselves against him the way the world sometimes seems to array itself against us. Yet he was silent and free of all resentment. He did not ignore evil; he handled evil. He did not say everything was good; he met an issue. Earlier he had said to Peter that he knew that Peter would deny him. He did not forbid Peter to do it. Jesus saw the problem and left the individual free.

There will always be people to hate, and there will always be enough fools to hate them, until we awaken the world to a spiritual consciousness. The people you do not like are a challenge to you. What another person thinks about you is none of your business. Your entire business is the operation of your state of consciousness. People may dislike you; they can do anything to you they want. It is not very important. Within you there is an integrity of the Spirit. Within you there is the capacity to look out at your world through your own state of consciousness and see it as good. You need to live in peace with yourself. That is why Jesus, in the 18th chapter of Matthew, said to Peter that he should forgive others not seven times but seventy times seven. For the other person's sake? No; for Peter's sake.

Jesus lived in a world which did not like him, but he prayed and liked the world. He lived among groups of people who said he was vile; and he calmly loved them enough to heal them. You can do this. You can go into your office tomorrow, and you can think, "No matter what anyone says unkindly to me, I am going to say in my own mind that there is not one word of Truth in it. I do not care. I believe that within these people is a spiritual possibility. I behold the Good in them. I behold the good in them." That is practical metaphysics. That is true forgiveness.

# You Can Be Healthy Today

*"I am one with all the wisdom, all the mind, all the health there is. I and the Father are one. I am Spirit."* The moment you become ill, it is because you have forgotten these truths about yourself.

VERY FEW PEOPLE think of their health as a spiritual activity. They think of it as being dependent upon such outer circumstances as rest, recreation, correct food and exercise. When you first contacted metaphysics, you discovered that there are several million people who really believe that the health of their bodies is the health of God. Health is as natural to man as his thinking, his feeling, or any other experience in life. It is normal to be healthy; it is abnormal to be sick. This is not only true of youth, it is also true of the adult.

A definition of health solely on the basis of body diagnosis is incomplete. You are mind, acting through body, in a world which you can always change. People are doing it all the time. Failures are changing into successes. Some people make greater sums of money each year. Others move into better homes. They are changing their worlds around them through an action of their minds. There is no other explanation. A shrewd businessman who increases his business and thereby brings greater profit to himself and to his employees is using his mind to do it. He is alert, keen and knows what to do—which is another word for inspiration. He changes his world through his use of mind.

You change your world through your use of mind. If it is only as simple a thing as purchasing an article for the home, your mind wanted it. Your mind took you to the store to get it. Your mind selected it. With your mind you decided whether to buy it or not and to order it delivered. Upon its delivery at your home you unpacked it, because your mind told your hands to do it. You looked it over to see if it was perfect. You put it in the place where you wanted it to be through the action of your mind directing your body. The entire transaction took place at two levels—at the directive level of mind and at the secondary level, where mind moved through form for results.

If your mind determines your world—and it does—then your mind must determine your body, because your body is a part of your world. Your body is a function of your mind, just as your income is, your job is, or your existence is, in the world of form. Your body in itself cannot create disease. Body, being intelligence subconsciously in action, of itself can never induce a conscious action. The subconscious can impress itself upon the conscious, but it cannot be the conscious. It cannot fulfill the functions of the conscious. The body that you are wearing at this moment is a body of subconscious intelligence which reacts as your conscious intelligence directs it.

Then why do you get sick? There are many schools of thought on this. The medical physicians give you the material reasons. The psychologists give you the emotional reasons. The theologian of orthodoxy says you become ill because you sin, but I see so many people sinning who do not get sick that I am suspicious of that theory. Sometimes there is no one healthier than a good sinner.

In our Science we say that sickness is a result of an unconscious negative conditioning over a period of time. The question which people ply us with more than any other, and every practitioner will bear me out in this, is "Why should I have this illness if I never thought of it?" You didn't think of it as "it," but you continually thought of some negative. Casual thoughts do not make you sick. Casual unimportant misdirection of emotions does not cause neurosis. It has to be deeper than that. Negative thinking over a period of many years can bring about a serious illness. Illness is the result of either conscious or subconscious negative conditioning over a period of time. That is what makes you sick. A consistent change of thought will make you well, because there is One Process, One Mind, One Law and One Good. You are using It with free will, and you may use It either way you want.

Jesus healed sick people. Elijah and Elisha in the Old Testament healed sick people. Interestingly enough, the disciples after the death of Jesus healed very few people. The later Church did little healing, and down through the years there have been minor healing groups and healing shrines. All of these have healed people, and they have healed through no material means.

I recently read a lengthy document, a study made by American psychologists at the healing shrine of Lourdes in France. They went there complete skeptics, and they came away about ninety percent skeptical. But they admitted on the eightieth page of this treatise, after stating how many people were not healed, that a small percentage of people with incurable diseases and with chronic ailments of years' standing had been healed in front of their own eyes through no material means. They went on to say that the few healings which they had witnessed in their six months' study were not the usual types which psychologists believe faith healing might cure. The cures were very few in number compared to the thousands who go to the shrine each year.

We do not know how many people Jesus could not heal. His biographers, like all biographers, wrote only the good. They would not admit that he had not healed everyone. Having been in the healing practice for twenty-five years, I am sure that Jesus did not heal everyone, but he did heal a great many.

Jesus told a chronic bed-ridden invalid to ''arise and walk.'' Immediately, the man was healed and actually walked. The thing which caused the man to arise and walk after thirty years of illness was an action in the mind of Jesus effective in the mind of the man. Something happened in the sick man's mind which was so dramatic, so definite, that it radically and instantly changed his subconscious patterns and he was instantly healed. Something Jesus was thinking became a fact within the man. I see no other answer, unless you go back to old-fashioned theology. Then you have a special man sent to earth in a peculiar way, healing a few people, uttering a few words, and ascending again to God. Such a theory takes spiritual healing out of reason and logic.

Jesus was one of the greatest spiritually minded men who have ever lived. He understood intuitively what you are now studying consciously. He realized that within himself was a center of Divine operation. At this center within he was unified with and was a part of an unlimited Intelligence. Not only that, he knew he could direct that Intelligence and that It would not return unto him void but would accomplish the thing whereto It was sent.

Jesus stood by the sick man and spoke to him. The man changed his thought, and with this correction of consciousness he was healed. But this was accomplished because Jesus thought something. Let's see if we can find out what it was that Jesus thought.

Jesus had told his disciples that the material world around him was a world of experience but not a world of limitation. Your world around you is pretty much what you make of it. It can be hard and boring; it can be difficult; or it can be heaven.

Jesus knew that the universe does not act upon man; man acts upon it. He realized that his consciousness (his thinking and his feeling) determined his experience. "For as he thinketh in his heart, so is he" (Proverbs 23:7). Jesus was the first person to completely act as though this were true. When you act as though the thing you believe is so, it will become so, because belief accepted sets the Law of Mind in action to produce the demonstration. You may believe in metaphysics and remain sick, poor, lonely, unhappy and fearful. Jesus realized that as he moved from the belief level to the knowing level and acted as though it were so, it had to be so.

As you cease merely believing that your mind is a spiritual function and use it as though it were, it will then produce the results of the Spirit. As long as you believe that your mind is spiritual only if you are giving a treatment, having a meditation, saying a prayer or reading a scripture, and that the rest of the time it is not spiritual, you have a double consciousness, and you have a double result in your world.

Jesus once said to the people who wanted to do everything

he did, "Are ye able to be baptized with the baptism that I am baptized with?"—meaning, have you cleansed your mind of all the reasons why Truth won't work? Then you will work It. In the 9th chapter of Luke, verse 23, we read, "And he said to them all, If any man will come after me, let him deny himself, and take up his cross daily, and follow me." Deny the power of any external condition to operate in you as authority. Take your problem, look it squarely in the face, and say, "There is not one word of truth in this situation and I refuse to accept it. I am not the victim of anything. I am pure Spirit." That is taking up your cross and following his ideas.

You have then moved from the belief level to the knowing level. You no longer say, "I believe in health." You say, "I am health." Jesus said, "I am God." Very few of you have the courage to say that to yourselves. You use the family name, you garnish yourself with human-mind excuses, and you rest in the complacency of material existence. That is why the sick are not healed and the sad remain unhappy. Not until they deny themselves the enjoyment of material excuses and face their problems, be it business, health or whatever it is, can they find healing.

Look your problem in the face, declare that it cannot be, for there is no room in you for it. There was no room in the inn for Mary and Joseph. The inn represents the crowded intellect, the human-mind reasoning, that is always so busy. But behind the inn is the stable, and it is there that your healing is born. The stable represents the simplicity of saying to a problem, "You are a liar," and saying to the solution, "I give you birth." This is your redemption out of the vagaries of your own false mental conceptions. Your true Christ health appears, and you behold the wonder of your healing.

# The Cause and Cure of the Common Cold

*Medicine treats disease.*
*We treat mental causation.*

## INTRODUCTION

YOU CANNOT AFFORD to have the common cold, viruses, sinus troubles, postnasal drips, etc. They are a tremendous waste of time, energy and money. They are of no value and they teach no lessons.

"Americans will spend Three Hundred and Fifty Million Dollars ($350,000,000.00) on the prevention and cure of the common cold during the year 1963." This statement, from market research authorities, published in the March 1, 1963, issue of *Forbes Magazine*, is shocking.

Another research report shows that twenty-two million, eight hundred thousand (22,800,000) Americans went to medical doctors in a single year to be helped and cured of the common cold. Twenty-two percent (22%) of this great number made at least a second visit to the doctor.

These statistics are shocking. In addition, there is no way of estimating the number of days men and women have lost from their work, the financial losses to corporations for these lost man-hours, nor the cost to insurance companies for temporary hospitalization.

All this adds up to a startling need for this booklet written by a man with several decades of factual experience in the field of Spiritual Mind Healing. That the common cold and its fellow-complaints will yield to spiritual/mental treatment is beyond question. Thousands of people in the last seventy-five years have used mental and spiritual methods with consistent success.

Mental-emotional causes of our physical ailments are increasingly accepted by the general public as the result of more than a century of metaphysical pronouncement and decades of psychosomatic studies in the medical field.

The spiritual scientist makes a claim far greater than does psychosomatic medicine. He states that all colds, viruses, forms of pneumonia, sinus difficulties, etc. are the result of emotional confusion in the subconscious mind of the patient. To receive results from the study of this booklet and from the application of the simple methods outlined in it, the patient must be willing to recognize the basic premise that colds are caused by oneself. They do not come from material or external causes. The weather does not cause colds. Overwork and fatigue do not cause them. Exposure to others with colds does not cause them.

There is only one cause of the common cold. It originates in the mental-emotional constitution of the individual. It is an outer expression of an inner hurt. When you know this and are able to admit to yourself that your mind and emotions alone have caused the cold, you can be cured by the spiritual ideas explained in the pages which follow.

## THE CAUSE

THERE IS NO material causation of colds. Whatever their form, whatever their medical description, they are the result of emotional confusion of some kind. This emotional causation is often unknown to the victim, as it is always subconscious.

You will probably find in the following possible subconscious emotional patterns one which fits your immediate past thinking and experience. I say immediate, as colds are not the result of long-standing confusions. They begin their appearance generally within a ten-day period from the time of the subconscious disturbance. They are always the result of sudden, often dramatic—and never permanent—emotional sprees, hurts or stoppages of self-expression.

Colds are usually caused by hurts, misunderstandings and unhappy situations in personal relationships. Things, offices, homes, etc. do not cause colds. Your reactions to people in these and other situations do. Neither do fears cause colds. Deep-seated fears will cause other types of physical disturbances, but not colds. Seek for your cause in your recent relationships with others, particularly relatives, fellow-employees, neighbors and friends. I often remark to patients: "Who is the matter with you?"

Read the following list carefully. No list is ever complete, but it will start you seeking the confused cause and will usually make you aware of the cause of your particular form of emotional-mental congestion, which the Law of the Subconscious is now manifesting as a cold or similar condition.

## THE CAUSES

### A Recent Argument

Any argument you clearly remember in which you became emotionally upset. Particularly any argument with a loved one. A job situation could cause colds if the argument involved a strong personality.

### A Recent Injustice

The feeling of being imposed upon. A feeling of not being wanted. Others are getting what you should have. Others are more loved. Some personal situation where you feel you are unjustly treated by a member of your family or loved ones or fellow-employees. Your reactions to quarrels with close friends.

### Emotional Confusion

A general term covering many areas of personal relationships. Your definite annoyance with a person. Your resentment at being dominated. Your feeling that your opinions are not respected. Bitter, quick quarrels with loved ones. "Blowing up" at home or in the office.

## Emotional Hurts

Not telling off the people who have hurt you. Hiding your hurt within yourself. Being the perfect lady or gentleman at all times. Refusal to see the faults of others, yet being hurt by these people. Trying not to admit the imperfections of relatives and friends. Not "blowing up," but priding yourself on self-control. Deep subconscious refusal to speak up for your rights.

## Emotional Brooding

Hiding your feelings from others through false pride. Maintaining a calm surface while boiling underneath. Gloomy thinking over a period of days or even hours. Feeling that no one appreciates you or wants you. Brooding in despair on minor hurts caused by other people. Brooding over your death. Making fantastic funeral plans to get even with those who have hurt you. Enjoying your brooding because it makes you feel a martyr.

## Sudden Rejection Feeling

"Nobody loves me. I am all alone in the world. No one wants me around anymore." Deep self-depreciation due to someone hurting you. Unconscious enjoyment of being hurt, as it makes you important to yourself. The hope that others will not accept you. Wanting others to understand how much they have hurt you.

## Wanting to Get out of an Obligation

Unconsciously making your subconscious lie for you. Easier to have a cold than say no to an invitation or a responsibility. Unconscious desire to avoid a situation or group you don't like.

## Uncompleted Metaphysical Projects

Not following through on a line of treatment until the demonstration is made. Congestion resulting from having made definite treatments toward a specific end, then changing your mind and not continuing. The idea starting to move toward manifestation gets bogged down, and congestion of consciousness results in colds.

## Miscellaneous Possible Causes

Emotional confusion, agitation, disturbance. Feeling of sudden loss. Jealousy, secret inner fight. Shocks, personal resentment. All the negative emotions taken to heart in the last ten days.

## Attention-Catcher

An unconscious means of getting attention. Also, a cold can break up monotonous routines of living. Gives you something to complain about to relatives, friends, and fellow-employees. A secret enjoyment of martyrdom to gain sympathy.

# THE CURE

SPIRITUAL MIND HEALING is accomplished through the use of specific denials and affirmations. Its whole purpose is to change patterns in the subconscious mind so that the inherent Spiritual and Perfect Man or Woman is again demonstrated. Treatment destroys evil and reveals the good that has always been latent in consciousness, for consciousness is God.

You do not treat to be rid of a cold. You treat to get clear on the Allness of God. As you treat, the subconscious negative pattern which caused, created and is maintaining the cold dissolves and the corresponding physical effect disappears. We do not treat evil, we treat to know God, and evil goes as the knowledge of God is revealed. The only thing needed to clear a cold is to clear yourself of the inner negative emotion which started it. You are not fighting, arguing or lying. You are announcing to yourself what you are in God.

As you announce to yourself what you are in God, you casually decline to believe any longer what your subconscious has been believing about the emotional hurt. You are not fighting a belief when you deny it. You are merely using the denial as a dismissal of the belief, and it goes. Your denial of the emotional congestion is not an admittance of its reality. It is merely saying that it has no existence in your subconscious mind.

A Spiritual Mind Treatment to clear a cold is a simple one. If possible, do it audibly. Follow these simple suggestions in the exact order they are given:

## THE METHOD OF TREATMENT

1. Begin by making audible statements convincing yourself of Perfect God, Perfect Man and Perfect Being.

2. Deny that there is any material causation. Deny any specific beliefs you may have, such as weather, overwork, fatigue or pressure. You are God's Creation and these cannot operate in or through you. They never have and they never will.

3. Deny that medical opinion is true. Don't let mercury in a thermometer determine whether you are sick or not. Your health in God cannot be diagnosed and opinionative. You are Spirit. Deny what others tell you is so. You look well. You

feel well, for you express the Life that is perfect. Deny that other people can talk you into sickness.

4. State a clear denial of the particular emotional pattern that you have discovered is the probable cause of the cold. Make clear in your thought that it cannot be so, for it is not spiritually true, therefore it cannot be real.

5. Now affirm the opposite of your denial. State that the person involved in your hurt is a spiritual being, a Divine Idea in the Mind of God. Keep thinking rightly of the person and the place and the situation that is involved in It.

6. State that all relatives, close friends, loved ones and employers or fellow-employees are true representatives of the Spirit of God. They are the means by which God reveals His goodness in your life. Keep on this way until you really feel it to be so—because it is so.

7. You are now ready to close your treatment. Reaffirm your faith in God, your faith in Truth. Declare you are Life, Love and Wisdom. Give thanks that you have never been sick, aren't sick now and never will be sick. State the Allness of God and then say a loud AMEN.

*What follows is a treatment for colds. Use it only to start a flow of ideas. It has no magic in it. It is neither perfect nor complete. It merely starts you thinking in the right direction.*

*After using this treatment, start declaring one of your own—using your own vocabulary. Be certain it is positive, honest and clear. Write it out if that helps. But don't be in bondage to written treatments nor to those of another person or teacher.*

*You are an individual in God. Be this by thinking out your own Treatments.*

## THE TREATMENT

THERE IS ONLY ONE GOD, ONE MIND, ONE TRUTH AND ONE REALITY. I AM THE ACTION OF GOD IN THE PERFECT ACTION OF GOD. I AM THE LOVE OF GOD IN THE LOVING PRESENCE OF GOD. THERE IS NO MATERIAL OR MEDICAL CAUSATION OF COLDS. GOD IS THE ONLY CAUSE AND THE ONLY EFFECT. I AM SPIRIT EXPRESSING AS SPIRIT BY MEANS OF A SPIRITUAL BODY RIGHT HERE AND RIGHT NOW. I KNOW THAT THE EMOTIONAL CAUSE OF MY MOMENTARY COLD IS NOW DISMISSED FROM MY SUBCONSCIOUS MIND. NO PERSON, SITUATION OR REACTION HAS CAUSED IT. IT CEASES AT THIS INSTANT. I LOVE EVERYONE. I CANNOT BE HURT. I AM NEVER MISUNDERSTOOD NOR REJECTED. I AM NEEDED, LOVED AND APPRECIATED BY RELATIVES, FRIENDS AND CO-WORKERS. I AM PERFECT LIFE, PERFECT HEALTH AND PERFECT VITALITY. I HAVE NO COLD. MY SUBCONSCIOUS IS NOW CLEAR OF ALL NEGATIVE EMOTION AND I AM PERFECT. I PRAISE THE GOD THAT IS, FOR I AM THAT GOD IN MANIFESTATION THIS MOMENT AND FOREVERMORE. AMEN.

# Money Is God in Action

*Money is God's Idea of circulation in my life.*

WE ARE DISCUSSING money. The people who have it want more; the people who don't have money want it. There isn't a person in the world who will admit to having too much money and who would not like to juggle his stocks and bonds to have a little more.

What is this money that we are discussing? We worry about its valuation. We have a curious mixture of doubt and fear in most of our thought of money. We seem to be confused. We do not know whether its value is dependent upon money as gold locked underground in Fort Knox, Kentucky or whether it is dependent upon the stock market. That, too, seems to affect

96

money. And we worry when other nations devaluate their currency, for fear it will affect our own country's money. So I think it would be a good idea if we discussed money and cleared our thought regarding it.

The last one hundred years have brought about what is called a scientific age. This scientific age has given us a great deal, but the average person considers it merely in terms of his own increased personal comfort. The sincere student of science discovers that back of this increased comfort there should also be an increased understanding of the world and of the universe of which this planet is only a small part. One of the things which our friends in the scientific field have done is to make us realize that the universe is a fluidic creation, an eternally flexible creation. It is always in a state of flux; it never stops or stands still for an instant. It is energy forever expanding itself. It is Intelligence forever finding new outlets for its own creative action.

As we view this Universe of infinity, eternity and activity, and consider our planet in relation to this great Cosmic order, we behold a universal field of right action. We might say that the first necessity for understanding the world in which we live is to understand it on the premise that it is activity; it is never static. See yourself in a fluidic universe, a flexible universe, a universe that is forever in process of change yet at the same time forever dominated and guided by a basic Intelligence, which is forever producing new forms, new creations, new experiences, all of which when seen rightly are good. If you can realize that, then you will deal with your universe as a flowing thing. Then you will deal with your prosperity as a flowing thing. You will immediately realize that the average person has stopped his own prosperity because he has concluded that prosperity is money in the bank, or money in investments, instead of seeing prosperity as a flowing thing, an inlet and an outlet of activity.

There is a universal pulse-beat. This great flowing, pulsating universe has its own measurements of stars and atoms, its own pulse-beat. You as an individual, taken physically, have your own pulse-beat which denotes to the nurse or the doctor the tempo of your circulatory system; but remember that it is a *circulatory* system—it is an eternal movement taking place in you. In a well person this circulation is in balance, always in right relationship. When your pulse is taken, no matter whether it is fast, slow or average, it is an indication of the tempo of your circulation.

Likewise there is a barometer, if we wish to call it that, for our national pulse-beat in economics. Many people pick up their morning or evening newspaper, and the first thing they read is the stock market page, the barometer of the pulse-beat of the financial day as it has been recorded. If the market goes down, they moan; if it goes up, they rejoice. They have become dependent for their feeling of prosperity upon a set of statistics presented to them by authorities in the financial field. I am citing these pulse-beats because each is indicative of circulation. The stock market is dependent upon buying and selling. It is a circulatory thing, just as the pulse of your own body is dependent upon the beating of your heart, the circulatory system and the moving of the blood throughout your body. All life is circulation.

When I begin to fear lack, and that often happens, I immediately begin to work on my own consciousness, not with the question of how I can make more money, but with the question, "What do I need to do to have money circulating in my world?" For prosperity is the circulation of money in my world. It is movement, it is an activity, it is a flow. I have often defined prosperity as being a state wherein I am always able to do what I want to do at the instant of time that I want to do it. In other words, if all the people attending a metaphysical lecture had sufficient money in their pockets to place a generous contribution in the offering plate and they had sufficient money in their pockets to have transportation home, then at that instant they would be prosperous, despite what their bank account revealed, because they would have what they needed to have to do the thing they wanted to do at the instant they wanted to do it.

The older theologies have been telling us, for as long as any of us can remember, that money is a dangerous thing, that money is an evil thing and that money is a sinful thing. In metaphysics we do not believe that. But there are countless good people who believe it, and I look at them in amazement, for while they believe that money is the root of all evil (which isn't what Jesus said), they are forever bothering their employers for a raise. If you believe that money is evil, then why work for it? Why use it? Merely go and live with some kind relatives and you won't need to bother about it.

Money is a vital part of the necessary circulatory system of this age. As it is a necessity for the economic health of all of us, it must be a spiritual idea. The moment you shift your attention from the concept that money is evil to the belief that money is wonderful, you will begin to have a greater circulation of money in your life. Anything we love increases, and anything we criticize moves out of our lives. The first step toward abundance is to love money. Why? Because it is the means which God is using at the present instant to maintain a circulation in your world of economics. But it must be a circulation. Therefore, watch out before damming it up, hemming it in or putting a fence around it, because the joker is still in that deck of cards. If you die one of these days, your relatives have a free-for-all with it. That is the joker for people who hoard money.

Circulation is necessary to my body if I am to keep on living. Circulation is necessary in the general field of economics if we are to have a healthy financial structure in this nation and in the world. Therefore, I can assume that circulation is necessary in my own bank account, in my own pocketbook, and more than that in my mental attitude about money. I must believe that I am in a universe which is self-sustaining. If I am in a universe which is self-sustaining, then I must be a part of it, and the creative process which causes the universe to be self-sustaining must likewise be in my affairs and cause my affairs to be self-sustaining.

The universe is saying to the mind of man that if he will be wise in his use of money, if he will be receptive to the idea of money, he will have money. For no good thing is withheld from those who love God, and money is good, but you have to believe that money is good. So correct your thought about money.

Next—we must be willing to live in a state of financial flux. We must be willing to live in a state of financial flexibility and meet it without fear. If we can do that we will have more money. If only there were doctors of money as there are doctors of bodies and doctors of the mind, for we need to be reminded often that we must be flexible in money matters. When the barometer on our bank account goes down, it is merely an indication that it will go up again, if we remain open to the idea of money.

You must sell yourself on money as a spiritual idea until it becomes an automatic subconscious pattern with you. You will find that the people who have the greatest freedom in money are the people who no longer have to think about money. They have arrived at a subconscious conviction that they will always have it. And they always do have money, because they are subjectively convinced of the fact. The people who have trouble in regard to money have not yet convinced themselves that they can live in this world and have the freedom and use of money. I do not mean millions of dollars; I mean enough to live more than comfortably.

You are going to say, "But, doesn't money come from work?" The answer is "No." There are business executives who work only two hours a day, or one day a week, and take a six-week vacation whenever they desire, and yet they receive enormous salaries. They receive their money because they are considered to be worth that much money. And the reason they are considered to be worth this much is that they have convinced themselves that they are worth it. When you are convinced that you are worth more money, walk up to your employer and say you want a raise, and you will receive it. But you will never get a raise if you merely want a raise but are not convinced that you are doing a better job than you did a year ago, that you are willing to watch the time-clock less, and that you are willing to be more active on the job. You will get your raise only when you are convinced in your own subconscious that you are worth it.

We must first convince our own minds. That is probably why every time people came to Jesus and needed his help, he asked them, "Do you believe?" If they said, "Yes," he said, "All right, it is done." Why? Because they had arrived at a point of self-conviction, and it was their own self-conviction which made the demonstration. Jesus could feed 5,000 people because he was convinced he could feed 5,000 people. He knew he could do it, so he did it. You don't know that you can do it, so you had better not try to do it. And don't infer that the scriptural story of the feeding of the 5,000 is allegorical, or that it is a myth, for you won't know that you too can do it until you have arrived at the same point of subconscious conviction which Jesus had realized. Money is a subjective conviction on the part of the individual.

Accept the idea of money and say, "All right, it is God's Idea of circulation [that is our definition—money is God's Idea of circulation], and I now subjectively accept the Idea of money. I accept this Divine Idea without limitation. I do not think of money in terms of any set amount. I think of it in terms of plenty to maintain me in ease and freedom of action.''

The reason that I suggest that you don't treat in terms of amounts is that wealth is a relative thing, and one fact about the Universal Mind is that it always gives plenty and to spare. I am weary of having just enough to meet my current bills. I want a little to spare. All right, that is the way the Universal Supply works. The Universal Intelligence works under a law of abundance without a secondary law of limitation. But most individuals attempt to work under a law of abundance with an unconscious pattern of limitation. So they do not have results. On the surface they say that they desire plenty of money, but their subconscious pattern is $100.00 a week. As the subjective pattern has more power than the temporary conscious-mind desire, they demonstrate $100.00 a week, while they could be demonstrating as much more as God wanted them to have. The Universe takes us at our valuation, and each one of us needs to increase the consciousness of our own valuation in money. As we do this, money starts to appear in our experience.

All spiritual treatment is an action of the conscious on the subconscious. Treat this way: ''Money is God's Idea of circulation. This Idea I accept. This Idea I now accept as the basis of all my financial affairs. I like money. I believe that it is God's Activity, that it is good. I use it with wisdom. I release it with joy. I send it forth without fear, for I know that under a Divine Law it comes back to me increased and multiplied.'' If you will use this treatment and subjectively accept it, you will be amazed at the results.

Money is a Spiritual Activity. It is good, it is wonderful, and we should love it. It is not filthy lucre, it is not sinful, it is not the devil's playmate—it is God in action. The stock market is a financial barometer. We do not condemn it, we do not criticize it, neither do we bless it; we merely leave it alone. We use it as an orderly part of our business world. We do not worry about the value of dollars, because whether values go up or down, we who are convinced within ourselves that we are worth plenty of money will always have it.

We will always have money, because the law of prosperity is based on the perpetual circulation of God's Ideas in the Infinite Mind.

This great circulation of thought is pouring into our consciousness and appearing in our world as cash on hand. This process goes on eternally, despite the value of a dollar or the value of a pound sterling. But the people who believe that their money is dependent upon the stock market, or believe that their money is dependent upon valuation, or believe that their money is dependent upon hours of work—those people are living under the bondage of limitation, and they do not demonstrate money. They demonstrate more worry, more watching, more fear, because that is where they have placed their attention. That is where they are setting up cause, so they reap a similar effect, because cause and effect are one.

If I devote my entire thinking, which is the creative power in my world, to worry about money, then the effect must be like unto the cause, and I only have more worry about less money. That is completely logical as well as completely true. Therefore it is necessary to take my attention from money as a necessity of life and think of it as a God-given Idea for life as a necessary part of the normal circulatory system of the present age. Say to yourself, "Isn't money wonderful! I'm going to release it with joy. I refuse to worry, for there is plenty more money for me."

I want to close this booklet with a specific mental treatment for money. I want you to be clear on this one idea. I am not giving you a treatment to increase your salary, I am treating for *money*. After you read and declare audibly this treatment for money; you must be willing to take it when it comes. If someone stops you on the street and invites you to a fine restaurant—go. Let your money come from any direction. I have known people who came to our practitioners' offices for a money treatment and, after the treatment was given, would go out and mingle with a group of friends. I would hear a friend say to one of them, "May I take you to lunch?" and he would say, "Oh no, I *couldn't* accept." Then why should he take a practitioner's time to treat him for money? If someone says to you, "I want to give you something," and it is at all usable, take it. If it isn't usable, take it anyway and give it to someone else, because that is the way bridge prizes circulate.

Remember that if money is God in Action, if it is a Spiritual Idea in your life, then you should welcome with joy anything resembling it. Be a little enthusiastic about money. Don't criticize anyone who has it. If you believe that someone down the street is getting money dishonestly—what of it? He is working under the law of his own negative mind and he will be stopped. Don't worry about it. It is none of your business, and don't criticize him. Think of money as being God in Action, and whenever you see large amounts of money, say to yourself, "Isn't that wonderful!"

This human mind of ours has its tricks of limitation, and it gives itself away every time. If I treat myself for prosperity and go out and criticize someone else because he has plenty of money, it doesn't make sense, does it? The mental work I have done is rendered ineffective because my own criticism of money has erased its value.

You are going to like money, because it is God in Action. You are going to use it with wisdom, release it in joy and know it will return to you increased. Say to yourself, "Wait a moment —I always have had enough money to meet my needs, and the Infinite Spirit is not going to stop my income at this point. There is no blockage in the universal system; the universe is always in a state of flux. If there is a block in the flow of money in my life, it must be a temporary human block which I have within my own consciousness. I now break that block. I accept money, appreciate money, use money and shall never again be afraid of money."

*Both riches and honor come of thee, and thou rulest over all; and in thy hand is power and might; and in thy hand it is to make great, and to give strength unto all.*

1 Chronicles 29:12

# TREATMENT FOR MONEY

I NOW SUBCONSCIOUSLY ACCEPT THIS TREATMENT. THERE IS ONLY ONE CREATIVE CAUSE, GOD. THERE IS ONLY ONE MIND, GOD. THERE IS ONLY ONE LIFE, GOD. THERE IS ONLY ONE SUBSTANCE, GOD. THIS PRESENT UNIVERSE IS THE GLORY OF GOD. IT IS A MOVING, FLEXIBLE, FLUIDIC CREATION. IT IS ALIVE WITH THE LIFE, THE ABUNDANCE, AND THE RICHNESS OF GOD. I ABIDE IN PROSPERITY. MIND CREATED ME IN ORDER THAT IT MIGHT ACT THROUGH ME. THEREFORE, I AM RECEPTIVE TO ITS ABUNDANCE. I AM RECEPTIVE TO ITS CIRCULATION IN MY LIFE IN THE FORM OF MONEY. MONEY IS GOD'S IDEA OF CIRCULATION IN MY WORLD OF FINANCE. I ACCEPT THIS IDEA COMPLETELY. I APPRECIATE THIS IDEA; I LIKE IT. MONEY BEING GOD IN ACTION IS ABSOLUTE GOOD; IT IS WHOLESOME. IT IS A BLESSING TO MAN, AND I AM NOW PROSPERED WITH IT. I HAVE NO FEAR OF LACK FOR I BELIEVE THAT I HAVE

PLENTY OF MONEY. IT IS GOD'S ACTIVITY IN MY WORLD. IT IS GOD'S ACTIVITY IN MY BANK ACCOUNT. IT IS GOD'S ACTIVITY IN MY INVESTMENTS. IT IS GOD'S AC- TIVITY IN EVERYTHING TO WHICH I LAY MY HANDS. THIS MONEY IS FLOWING, THIS MONEY IS FREE. I DO NOT ATTEMPT TO LOCK IT UP. I DO NOT PUT A FENCE AROUND IT. IT IS GOD'S MONEY. I LET IT FLOW IN, I LET IT FLOW OUT. AS I RELEASE IT, I KNOW THAT IT COMES BACK TO ME PRESSED DOWN, SHAKEN TOGETHER AND RUNNING OVER. "THE LORD IS MY SHEPHERD; I SHALL NOT WANT." I AM NOW FREE IN MONEY. I REJOICE IN IT. I APPRECIATE IT, AND I THANK GOD FOR IT. I HAVE MONEY FOREVERMORE. AMEN.

> *A dollar is a miraculous thing. It is a man's personal energy reduced to portable form and endowed with powers the man himself does not possess. It can go where he cannot go; speak languages he cannot speak; lift burdens he cannot touch with his fingers; save lives with which he cannot directly deal, so that a man busy all day downtown can at the same time be working in boys' clubs, hospitals, settlements, childcare centers, all over the city.*
>
> Rev. Dr. Harry Emerson Fosdick

*If they obey and serve him,*
*they shall spend their days in prosperity*
*and their years in pleasure.*

Job 36:11